To Graham " Xmas 81"
Love
Denise

**Howie Meeker's
Hockey Basics**

Howie Meeker's Hockey Basics

Howie Meeker

Prentice-Hall of Canada Ltd.

Scarborough Ontario

Howie Meeker's Hockey Basics

© 1973 by Prentice-Hall of Canada Ltd.

Published by Prentice-Hall of Canada Ltd.,
Scarborough, Ontario.

Prentice-Hall, Inc., Englewood Cliffs, New Jersey
Prentice-Hall International, Inc., London
Prentice-Hall of Australia, Pty., Ltd., Sydney
Prentice-Hall of India, Pvt., Ltd., New Delhi
Prentice-Hall of Japan, Inc., Tokyo

ISBN 0-13-444257-1

Design by Peter Maher

Printed in Canada

2345   77 76 75 74

To Grace,
who has served every
penalty imaginable for
my interest in hockey,
with grace.

Acknowledgements

There would have been no book without the editing of my brother, Ken Meeker. Instructional books, of any sort, are not always the easiest to read. The insights and ability provided by Ken in editing the manuscript has, in my opinion, put the sugar coating on the instructional pill.

The background material for the drills was acquired through years of work in hockey schools in the Maritimes, with Roly J. McLenahan, Director of Sports and Recreation, Department of Youth and Welfare, Fredericton, N.B.; Dr. John Meagher, Professor of Physical Education, University of New Brunswick; and Professor Vance Toner, Director of Athletics, University of Moncton.

Many of my theories of developing skating power from balance originated with Jack Belec, professional figure and power skating instructor at a hockey school in St. Andrew's New Brunswick, during the summer, 1969. The Avalon Consolidated School Board, St. John's, Newfoundland, by giving the opportunity to work with 1,800 boys, helped me to lay the groundwork.

Buddy Blom was extremely helpful in providing tips for goaltenders.

The CBC sports team, who collaborated on the film, helped greatly in organizing the material for the book.

Howie Meeker

Contents

Introduction

Canadians should have learned at least one thing from the Canada-Russia hockey series of 1972. Unless there is a drastic change in our approach to the game, we're not going to be Number One much longer.

Canada invented ice hockey and I suppose it was understandable that we thought our professionals were the best in the world. When the pros just barely won that historic series with Russia, a lot of Canadians were pretty badly shaken up. A bunch of comparative newcomers showed us, among other things, that you don't pass stiff exams without doing a lot of homework.

And that, dear hockey fan, is what this book is all about. Homework. Going back to hockey's primary school (to which most of us never went) and learning the ABC's, the three R's, or whatever else you call basic training.

Because it's something I never had. Oh I learned enough about hockey to spend eight years playing in the National Hockey League and several more coaching professional teams. But it was not until after my professional career, when I started working with children, that I discovered the real guts of the game: why many kids' skates are junk; why a hockey stick can be kids' biggest handicap; why no youngster can be a good skater without learning balance.

I had to learn, by observation, the simple mechanics of developing power in a skating stride. I tried to figure out why a kid stops thinking when he starts moving. Only then did I realize that most Canadian boys never had a hope of reaching the N.H.L., because of the haphazard way they broke into the game.

So then I began a meticulous inspection of the boys' skates, sticks and protective equipment, and devised drills for teaching the basic skills. I wanted to create a learning experience that would be of value to all young hockey players, whether they had big league ambitions or not.

Next came a look at the Russian hockey machine when it came to Canada, and a closer look on the

subsequent trip to Russia. In Moscow, I spent all my spare time tracking down Russian training methods for children. My eyes bugged out. The Soviets had beaten us to it by at least fifteen years and had a basic hockey program miles ahead (in many aspects) of anything I was aware of here.

These were the hockey kindergartens that produced players such as Aleksandr Yakushev, Valeri Kharlamov, Anatoli Firsov and Vladislav Tretiak. The Russians theorized that with the right training, nearly any kid with average talent who really wanted to, could make the big time. It would be many years before they could prove it, but in the meantime, it was a good philosophy with which to work.

They compressed Canada's century of hockey experience into twenty years or so. To do that, they had to organize a system from the ground up. They did that, and they did it magnificently. In Canada meanwhile, the amateur hockey system is still in shambles.

I am convinced that Canadian coaches, parents and even kids have put so much importance on the glory of winning that the necessities of fundamental training have been shoved into the bleachers. Just watch many parents at minor league games, and you'll see what I mean—Mom and Dad hollering for goals while their eight-year-old youngster tries desperately not to fall on his keester when shooting the puck.

That poor little tyke isn't ready for a shot on goal yet; he's not even ready to take part in a passing play. He should still be out in a mad scramble with kids of his own ability, scrimmaging for the puck and having a ball unhindered by rules and whistles. There's no better way to get the feel of those rigs on his feet and that piece of wood in his hands. He will get pushed, kicked, punched and maybe cut, and he'll love every minute of it.

There's lots of time to teach a boy game tactics when he reaches his teens. But our priorities are topsy-turvy, and it's time we straightened them out.

To me, hockey is still the greatest game in the world. But it requires more skill, co-ordination and dedication than many young men are prepared to give. It's no wonder a boy gets discouraged when he finds himself in a game that demands something he doesn't have—solid physical and mental preparation.

This whole country was on the brink of despair during the Canada-Russia series, but we managed to pull that one out of the fire. Still, I don't think we have learned that big lesson; so far there's been little more than lip service paid to good basic training.

My hockey basics take a boy only as far as skating, using the stick properly, and knowing what to do with the puck when he gets it. While this to me is the most important part of his training, it is still just the beginning. There's a wonderful game ahead.

We have no choice now but to turn back to the fundamentals of the game. After we do, there will be thousands of kids lined up for their crack at a trip to Moscow.

Picture Credits

Grateful acknowledgement is made to the following for permission to reproduce their photographs on the pages listed below:

Dan Ballioti, pages 129, 131, 132-133, 134, 135

The CBC, page 22

Rene Ohashi, cover and all drill photos

Toronto Star, pages 14, 138

Terry Waterfield, chapter opening photos

Howie Meeker's Hockey Basics

1
Playing Equipment

Skates: The Most Important Basic

There's not much point in any of us going further with this game, unless we get one thing straight *right now*. Unless the boy has a good pair of skates he is wasting his time and yours. 'Good' doesn't necessarily mean expensive, as you'll see later. If you notice that I keep coming back to this point, there's a good reason. You had better get the message. *Quick.*

Skates provide support, mobility and protection. At this stage of a boy's development, support is of prime importance. It may surprise you, but it's my opinion that there are no such things as weak ankles. If your boy's ankles are bent at a 45 degree angle when he first goes on the ice, it's your fault, not his.

Consider that all his life he has worn shoes with soles three to four inches wide to support his weight. Now you are putting him on two strips of steel, one-eighth inch wide, and when he goes over on his ankles you cluck sadly and mutter "too bad, weak ankles". What else can you expect? You're asking him to balance just as well on one-eighth inch of steel as he does on those big clodhoppers he has worn all his life.

In my experience, maybe one boy in 150 has defective ankles that may need some special attention. The other 149 have defective parents who should have some special attention in the form of a well-aimed

boot in the keester for putting their kids into two pieces of junk and expecting them to perform.

You would understand why I feel so strongly about this if you could share with me an almost daily experience. A boy with good potential has been struggling with the balance and skating drills, but just can't seem to get the hang of it. He becomes frustrated, embarrassed; his confidence wilts. Then I convince his parents that the boy's new $19.95 skates are either too big or lack support. The boy gets properly outfitted (I'll explain how later) and the many parents who have witnessed the difference are flabbergasted. I have some idea how they feel, for the look of delight on the boy's face, when he realizes he's not a clumsy idiot after all, sends a tingle up my spine.

O.K., the skate must have support in the *counter*, which is the heel area of the skate, and in the ankle area. Notice the cardboard counter of the low priced skate (1), revealed by

1

cutting away the side leather. Many manufacturers are moving toward making the skate boot of plastic, so that this most crucial area gets proper support. Finding a pair that provides support (plus a good steel blade) in the lower price range–$11.95 to $14.95–isn't easy, but there are a few brands available.

The blade is only second in importance to the boot. If you ever get a chance, watch the average parent buy a pair of boy's skates. The boot gets some attention, but it's new, shiny, and stiff, so it must be good. It's the blade they find fascinating. Hold it to the light . . . see it shine. Run a finger down the edge . . . feels sharp. Heft it in your hand . . . feels sturdy. Hold the skates at arm's length and look knowledgeable. Check that blade once more, because after all, that's what makes the kid go like Gordie. Got a nice, clean, zingy–and somewhat danger-ous–look about it. Now nod, mutter-ing something about the price these days. For $11.95 you can't be too careful. Give 'em another heft, just to make sure it's exactly what Tommy wants, and head for the checkout. Poor Tommy.

The parent we described buying skates has probably condemned his child to the two biggest handicaps of a young hockey player:
- skates too big
- blades too soft

I have about 1,800 boys playing in a minor hockey league system and I would say that I check about a thousand pair of skates every year. I

look particularly for skates that are too large and counters that are too soft. It's difficult to believe, but from 75% to 80% of the boys have one or both problems.

You may argue, ''so what, maybe most of those kids are out there just for fun—call it recreation. Who cares if they go over on their ankles just as long as they can bash a puck around and fluke the odd goal?''

You're right on one count. At this age the kids should be out there primarily for fun. But even if they never make an organized midget or juvenile league, that's no reason why they shouldn't become good skaters. Skating is a recreation that can and should be continued until long after the old age pension cheques arrive. Besides, a good teen-aged skater who has never held a stick in his hand makes out just as well with the girls at the local skating sessions as the hockey player does. Just call it a fringe benefit, Dad.

Support

An educated guess is that about half those kids with inadequate skates did not try them on before purchase. They are victims of buying by 'size', an experience that can turn an unconcerned shopper into a rabid consumer rights advocate. We're dealing with the purchase of skates for boys up to 12 years, size 12 to about size four, in a price range from about $9.95 to $19.95. The first problem you will encounter is a lack of standardization in size. In other

24

words, 'Mac's Marvels' in size three are the same as 'Speedy Specials' in size four.

There is one other factor to consider. A size five in a $19.95 skate may be larger or smaller than a size five in a $29.95 skate, *made by the same manufacturer*, because the *last* differs. The *last* is the mould of the skate, from which the boot of the skate is cast. This *last* varies for the same *size* skate in different price ranges. So always try on every pair of skates you're considering.

I think mothers buy most skates these days. The old man is usually too busy at work, or watching TV, or he's afraid to accompany his number one son for fear the kid will learn that despite the old guy's tales of hockey prowess, he really doesn't know a thing about skates except where to take them for sharpening.

So while Tommy is at school, Mom jumps into the car or grabs a bus to the nearest shopping centre. The chain store there should have shelves lined with skates—probably on 'special' too.

That's mistake number one. The chain store may have a lot of skates, and maybe some good ones. But try to find a clerk to help you. However Mom's lucky and finds a young lady in the skate department . . . checking her makeup in the anti-shoplifting mirror.

"Yes Ma'am, we have a wide variety of skates. What price range are you interested in?"

"Well, not too expensive. After all, he's growing so fast he'll only be wearing them a year or so."

"What size does he take?"

"Oh . . . he wears size two now, so if I get size three maybe he'll get an extra year out of them."

Chances are, if Mom knew what to ask for, the girl would not know what she was talking about. On the other hand, if the clerk knew her job, she would suggest that Mom bring Tommy along and fit him properly. The store may have a good skate in stock, but neither Mom nor the clerk will recognize it.

If I'm going to tell you what to ask about and look for in a skate, you must shop in a place where they know what you're talking about. If there's a sporting goods store in your town, go there. If there's a shop that specializes in hockey equipment only, better still, but these are found only in the bigger cities.

Now your average sporting goods store in your average town may not be the place where Mom feels most at home. There's likely to be an aroma of leather and gun oil instead of the popcorn and perfume odour of most department stores. That scruffy looking customer in the corner may just be the best trout fisherman in the country. Expressions like 'muzzle velocity' and 'tapered glass ferrule' are occasionally heard. And (while I'm still in nostalgic flight) there has to be a middle-aged, slightly chubby, partly bald clerk just the other side of the jockstrap display. Don't worry about the jockstraps for another few years and head for that clerk.

Now tell the guy you want a pair of skates for the little kid with you, who by this time is clutching two dry flies in one hand and an open bottle of deer musk in the other. Tell him they should have a boot that holds his ankles as firmly as a vise, blades that will hold an edge for six hours of skating and a price tag that will not break the piggy bank. Even if that's all you know, the guy has the message.

If he is conscientious, he can fill your order for around $13.95, give or take a dollar. Don't get me wrong, you can find the same clerk in many chain stores. It's just that the chances are much better in a specialized store which is probably owner-managed. If the business is more than a couple of years old, the owner is smart enough to recognize Mom as a prize customer. If Mom gets a square deal on Tommy's skates, she may keep coming back for the rest of his gear as the young-ster grows . . . until Tom's ego gets big enough for him to decide it's time for a jockstrap and cup. But then, despite the pill, there is likely to be Geoff, and even Suzanne to outfit.

You told the clerk you wanted support. The only place Tommy needs support is in the counter and around his ankles, not around his toes or arches.

Most low-priced skates have counters made of pressed cardboard, or cheap leather that is not much better than cardboard. This may feel quite stiff or sturdy at first; but when put under any kind of strain, particularly when wet, the material either breaks, cracks or softens. Whatever happens, the skate loses any heel support it had and is useless. Finished. Kaput. There is no remedial action you can take. Pitch them out.

To illustrate, go get the skates your youngster is wearing now. Grasp the counter area from behind and pinch the two sides together. Twist them from side to side. If they are soft, limp or pliable, I'll bet you thought your young skater had weak ankles. His ankles bend when skating or turning, right?

If the counter feels stiff and requires considerable force to bend from side to side, the skate, if the correct size, should be providing good support. Remember, there are no weak ankles, only weak skates, or poorly-fitted skates.

Trying this test on a new pair of children's skates may or may not be useful. If the counters on a pair of new skates in the store feel soft, then discard them automatically. If they feel firm, or stiff, you must determine if the stiffness is perma-nent or temporary. You can't ask the clerk to soak a skate in water to see if the counter goes limp, but you can ask him how it's made.

The skate should have polyur-ethane or some other kind of strong plastic support built into the counter, the base area of the skate. There is one manufacturer of skates that has this extra feature built in, and these skates provide tremendous support.

The Blades

Before Tommy tries on his new skates, there is one more thing to check. I wish there was some simple guide for parents who are looking for a good blade. But there's not, and you pretty well have to go by price. Generally the higher-priced skates have a higher carbon content in the steel of the blade. As the price comes down, so does the quality of the steel, and the proportion. The carbon content, along with the hardening process, determines how long the blade will hold a sharp edge.

Are the blades *casehardened* or *through-hardened*? In a case-hardened blade, just the outside is coated with hard, good-quality steel. The stuff inside may be called steel but it has the characteristics of lead. It's like a reverse sandwich, a slice of bread between two pieces of tin. The blade is actually made from one sheet of uniform (but low) quality steel which goes through a special process that hardens the outside layers only.

Steel with a low percentage of carbon can be given a hard surface by increasing the amount of carbon at the surface so that it will respond to heat treatment. There are several methods of carburizing or case-hardening. It's a normal industrial process, but has no place in skate blades.

The term through-hardened is self explanatory. You want good steel through the entire blade. The fact that a child may wear them for only a year or two is irrelevant.

The sporting goods store you patronize may have a skate exchange department. When Tommy outgrows his skates you should be able to trade them in on a new pair. Likewise, once you know what to shop for, you should be able to pick up second hand skates in the smaller sizes at quite a saving. A used skate with a good stiff counter will still provide plenty of support, and there should be plenty of blade left. You will have to rely on the brand name or salesman's word for the quality of steel in the blade.

Above all, realize that second hand skates are not a disgrace. A good quality skate will outlast the amount of usage it gets from six kids, unless some ham-handed skate sharpener butchers the blades. Just apply the same rules of purchase to used skates as to new ones. It breaks my heart to see parents who can't afford it, continually buying new skates for their youngsters, when they can buy the same, or better quality, in a used skate at one-third the price.

The Fit

We're satisfied now with the quality of the boot and blade of Tommy's next pair of skates. So put them on him. You may start with the same size as the shoe he's wearing, but, as I have said, it may not mean very much in a skate size.

First, make sure Tommy is wearing just one pair of light weight socks. That's all, just one pair. Many parents put two or three pair of socks on their youngsters to prevent cold feet. But if the skates are fitted and laced properly, there will be no further problem with cold feet. Several pair of socks will usually cancel out any support built into the skate by building up too much soft padding between the skate counter and the flesh. The parent or child tries to take up the slackness by tightening the laces, which cuts off the circulation of blood, and causes the cold feet. So you have the same problem all over again.

You have probably gathered by now the reason why I forbid kids in my hockey schools to wear skates that are too large. No matter how many pair of socks they wear to take up the extra space, there's no way they can get the support necessary to perform anywhere near their full potential. Simply put, the more socks worn, the less support received from the skates. Without support, skating becomes hard work, not fun.

Back to Tommy's fitting. Parents quickly learn that kids' feet come in all shapes, sizes and proportions, from long and narrow to short and stubby. The youngster with a short stubby foot has a better chance of getting a good fit in skates. His feet will be wider and can be cupped more snugly by the ankle area of the boot. A boy with a long, narrow foot must get longer skates with a correspondingly wider heel cup and ankle space. Consequently, his narrower ankle and heel will leave far too much slack in the counter, even

when the skate is tightened.

The problem is that few kids will recognize this fault when trying on skates. When the skate is tightened, a kid can feel the ankles gripped securely, and is not aware that his heel could slip one-quarter to one-half inch to each side. But with a little imagination you can see the result when he skates—with his heel sliding around inside the counter area, he will be as wobbly as a new-born calf.

If your boy does have a narrow foot problem, and you have no choice but to buy skates with heel slack, there is a way out. Remedy the problem by having your local shoemaker put additional support into the ankle area. I'll enlarge on that later.

Many of these points may seem minor, but when combined with other factors—too many socks, soft counters, improper lacing—the result could be a major disaster.

When slipping the skate onto Tommy's foot you will probably have to use some force to get the foot settled in properly. Then the boy's natural reaction is to stand up and stamp the foot lightly just to make the final adjustment. Stop him right there, before he stands up, and make him bang the heel of the skate on the floor once or twice. He does this by pointing the toe in the air and striking the rear point of the blade on the floor, as he would when trying to chip a hole in the ice. I should not have to remind you not to try it on a terrazzo or concrete floor.

This action settles the heel back into the heel cup of the skate. If you look at a skate from the side, you will notice a definite protrusion at the back, for the heel. It's quite possible that when Tommy slips his foot into the skate he will jam his toes to the front and then settle his weight on the ball and heel of the foot. After all, this is the way he puts on his shoes. If he does this with skates, there could be a considerable gap between the back of his heel and the inside of the heel cup, which, if not noticed, can lead to many problems later. Tell the boy to make this heel adjustment *every* time he puts on skates.

With the heel settled in place, lace up the skates and have Tommy stand up. (Lacing is extremely important and is discussed later.) While the lacing holds the heel securely in the cup, determine if the boy's toes are touching the front, or toe, of the skate. In an ideal fit, the boy's toes are one-quarter inch clear of the toe of the boot. If before lacing, with the heel touching the back of the skate, he is also touching the front with his toes, take one-half to a full size larger. Remember, tap the heel snugly into place. Lace up. Stand up. If the toe then touches the front, buy a half to a full size larger. If the toe is clear of the front, the fit should be o.k. Finally, Tommy has his skates.

Leather Inserts

Lets look at what you have. Primarily, you have purchased a boot that should hold his heel as rigidly as a doctor's cast holds a broken foot. The cast resembles the skate boot further in that it does not require tightness to do its job.

When Tommy is standing, he will go over somewhat on his ankles inside the skate boot. This is normal. There may also be a small degree of tilting above the top edge of the skate boot and this too is normal. He should be able to lift his toes up and down freely and turn them from side to side.

When Tommy tries to bend his ankles inward and outward, a small fold of leather develops in the ankle area. Take the skates off and add leather inserts. Then the ankle area should be as firm as the counter. Folds or ripples of leather near or above the counter area are to be expected in almost all leather and nylon skate boots. It's not unusual, but it must be corrected because too much leather above the counter means not enough support, even with tight lacing. Get those inserts.

Here's something that is going to surprise you. If Tommy's skates are properly fitted, and have additional support from inserts in the ankle area, lace just the top three eyelets of each boot, draw them in tightly and tie them. Then send him out on the ice and watch him skate away. No problems. Pulling the top three eyelets tight gathers in all the loose leather around the ankle area and gives you the necessary support for skating. Assuming he already knows how, Tommy will be able to skate extremely well with just those top three eyelets laced tightly. Of course it will put additional strain on his feet and they're going to be pretty tired after a scrimmage, but it illustrates that you need to lace a well-fitted pair of skates tightly only in the top three eyelets.

So, except for lifting his toes up and down, and pointing them from side to side, Tommy's ankles should be immobilized. When you have accomplished this much, breathe easier. This may be overstating it slightly, but from here to the N.H.L., it's downhill all the way. That's exactly how strongly I feel about starting any youngster off in this game.

I could cry when I think of the weeks and months of wasted time when I first started working with boys and could not figure out why all the experts' drills were not working. After all, I was taught to skate by Boston's famous 'Kraut' line– Dumart, Schmidt and Bauer–who lived in my neighbourhood. I was somewhat over two years old at the time, a cushion tied on my keester, pushing a kitchen chair around the backyard rink. I should have learned everything there was to know in the years since, but it wasn't until I started teaching children that I realized that neither most of the men I played with nor I had a good basic training.

After a long, frustrating period with children I began to question the old wive's tale about weak ankles. I realized that all kids have strong ankles, but not quite strong enough for that transitional period from shoe soles to steel blades. The strength comes, of course, after varying lengths of time, but for several years all kids need unyielding ankle support.

Here's another curious flaw that sometimes occurs in skates. I once had a youngster with well-fitting skates and leather inserts in the ankle area, who went over on his ankles every time he performed even the simplest drill. On looking at the skate sole at eye level, I noticed that the blade was not centred on the sole—it was on a diagonal. Similarly, the sole and blade did not meet at a 90 degree angle—the boot was tilted away from the blade!

This flaw is not always the fault of the manufacturer. A hardskating kid using $13.95 skates with cheap, rubber insoles can do the same damage. We solved the problem by purchasing good skates ($24.95) and adding leather inserts for extra support.

A good, safe attitude to hold toward boys' skates is that they are potential junk. Despite your careful shopping and fitting for Tommy's skates, keep an eye on them as they get broken in. If the material in the counters is inferior after all, they will eventually break down under pressure or moisture. Then the boy will start wobbling or skating on his ankles again. Check the boot again with your hand. The once rigid sides will be soft and flexible.

At this point you have only one

choice. Get a refund or exchange from the retailer. With slack counters, the skates are useless. No extra support can be built into this area.

Take them back to the store and raise hell. Politely at first, and then with increasing vigour if there is any resistance. Your case is quite simple. The manufacturer has distributed a product that claims to do one specific job—enable the wearer to skate properly. With the skate in question the wearer cannot perform properly. Therefore the equipment cannot do the job for which it is intended, and is inferior. It's a bad product. You should demand a refund or exchange.

There is of course a price limit below which you cannot fairly go. I know at least one manufacturer who makes a skate that lives up to my specifications and sells in the vicinity of $13.95. If you pay much less than that for a pair of skates, except on sale, you can't reasonably demand any kind of performance from them, or expect a retailer to take your complaints seriously.

I am convinced that there are manufacturers of boys' skates who still think the only purpose of the boot is to hold the blade on the foot. Perhaps when the public starts to insist that boot quality come first, the manufacturer will get his priorities straight. Getting stuck with an inferior blade only means continual sharpening. An inferior boot can seriously retard, and in many cases completely discourage, a young-

ster's hockey ambitions.

As I have said, when a skate's counters go soft, you have to consider them useless. But if the skate lacks support in the ankle area because of excess or inferior leather, they can be repaired.

During my years of teaching skating and hockey, we have encountered the problem of poor support so often that we have had to develop our own skate modification. Remembering what Toronto Maple Leaf trainer Tommy Naylor once did for my skates and working with Howard Williams, a local shoemaker, we have perfected a set of leather inserts that can restore excellent support to any pair of skates with good counters. (2) (3) They are made of tapered, high-quality leather that will not break down under pressure and moisture, and are glued and sewn into each side of the ankle area in the skate boot. The pictures should provide enough information for any competent shoe-

2

3

maker to install the inserts.

The inserts are useful in several circumstances. If a boy has narrow feet and heels, making it difficult to find a boot that fits snugly, the inserts will take up the extra room in the ankles and heel areas. He will then have all the support he needs.

In any skate that is just slightly too large, when it is not economic to buy new skates, the inserts are the ideal way to make the skate fit where it counts most.

I strongly recommend that any parent who has the slightest doubt about the supportive quality of a new pair of skates, should have the inserts put in immediately. In fact, all brands for boys up to 14 years, regardless of price, need additional support in the ankle area. Leather supports for everyone is a great idea. It makes skating easier and more fun.

Now that we've talked you into leather inserts, there could be a flaw

in them! Many kids with bony ankles get sore spots from new leather inserts, because the sock strap around the foot, which is usually double-stitched with a big seam, rubs against the new, hard leather insert, irritating the ankle area.

If this is the case, slip the strap off and tuck it up behind the calf of the leg until the insert moulds itself to the ankle. If the sore spot persists, cut a doughnut from a piece of sponge rubber and place it over the ankle to relieve the pressure. For more direct action, wet the leather with a damp cloth and pound it a few times with a hammer.

In recent years we have put well over 2,000 supports into boys' skates. About one-quarter of these boys developed a sore area for a day or so, and needed a doughnut.

One word of warning: if the sore spots are not treated with a doughnut when on the ice and a bandage when off, the skin will break, making skating painful and uncomfortable for weeks.

The results of this extra support are quite startling. I run three hockey schools, two in Newfoundland and one in Stanstead, Quebec. In Newfoundland, if the school opens on Monday, applicants must register on the previous Saturday and bring all their equipment for inspection.

I spend most of my time checking skates for all the points I have mentioned previously, and I'm not ashamed to admit I'm a real stickler. Twenty out of 25 boys show up with skates that are too large. Most of the used skates that turn up have gone soft in the ankle area.

The new, grossly oversized skates are sent home immediately, with the boys, along with instructions on how to get a proper fit. The older skates, and the new ones that are close to fitting snugly, are shipped off to the shoemaker over the weekend to have additional supports put in the ankles. By Monday morning, every boy in the hockey school will be starting with at least every advantage a skate can give him. And the kid with $12.95 skates, in which extra ankle supports have been installed, has the same chance as the kid whose Dad can afford $40 for skates.

If a boy's skates are too large, or too soft in the ankles, he is wasting his time and mine at the hockey school. And if a parent refuses to co-operate in getting better equipment, he is wasting his own money plus the boy's time and our effort.

When the boy is fitted out with good skates, he immediately becomes teachable. And it's our neat little secret that just by insisting on proper skates, we have already improved his skating by from 35% to 40%. How's that for results without even taking him on the ice, or without one minute's worth of instruction?

Once we start instruction we can concentrate on teaching skills only, and the results start coming pretty fast. Two weeks of hard work by everyone involved can improve the boy's skating by a further 50%, and

only then does the student have a clean chance at becoming a really good skater.

Lacing

When the foot goes through the full cycle of striding on skates and developing power, the tendons on top work up and down, and the Achilles tendon that runs up the back of the foot from the heel works in and out. (4) Too many people

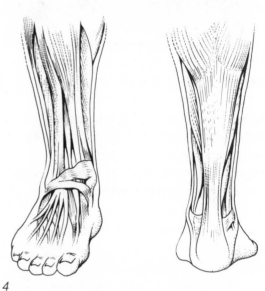

4

restrict the movement of these important tendons when lacing their skates, because they draw the laces too tightly from the bottom eyelets right to the top of the boot.

I have already mentioned one result of lacing too tightly—cold feet. Under normal skating conditions, I don't think it's possible for a boy with properly laced boots to get cold feet. But when the blood circulation is restricted or stopped, the result is inevitable.

When lacing lower-priced

children's skates, start with the second eyelet from the bottom. The toe cap in most cheaper models is not plastic or fibre, but a lower grade leather material. If you lace the first eyelet, which is usually over the end of the toe cap, the continuous pressure over a length of time will eventually break down the cap and force it in on the boy's toes. This can be very uncomfortable, even painful, and the boy may not realize what is causing it. So skip the first eyelet and start lacing with the second.

The number of eyelets on skate boots, depending on size, varies from about eight in the smallest size to 11 or so in the men's sizes. It's difficult to give a hard and fast sequence of lace tensions, so we will put it this way.

A size three boy's skate may have nine eyelets. The bottom three are over the ball of the foot; the next three are over the arch and the tendons on top of the foot; the top three eyelets are in front of the ankle.

The number may vary somewhat, depending on the size and brand of the skate. But whatever the number, break them down into these three categories:

- The eyelets over the ball of the foot, just behind the toes, that (looking from a side view) run almost parallel to the ground.
- The eyelets over the front curve of the ankle that, when tightened, exert pressure on the arch and the front tendons of the foot.
- The eyelets at the top of the skate

boot, in the ankle area. Lace the skates in the cross lace manner in which you lace your shoes; avoid loop lacing. In cross lacing, the laces don't stay rigidly tight. Tight lacing can be a disadvantage when a boy starts to skate, because his foot readjusts inside the boot with motion, and the loop lace maintains the initial unequal pressure of the lacing. With cross lacing, the laces slip to adjust in motion, keeping the pressure equal at each eyelet.

The laces through the bottom set of eyelets, over the ball of the foot, should be pulled with a moderate tension, so they are snug. All you need to do here is take up the slack in the skate boot so there is no loose leather around the foot. The only thing you accomplish by pulling them tightly is cutting off the blood circulation.

The next, or middle set of eyelets are very important. Too much pressure here interferes with the movement of those vital tendons on the front of the foot and can actually inhibit foot move-ment while skating. Pressure that is strong enough to squeeze the tendons will also restrict the blood supply and affect the arch of the foot. Luckily the arch has a warning signal that makes itself felt in the form of pains on the inside of the foot. The first time a boy complains of pains in this area, explain the cause and other probable results of tight lacing—

restricted tendon movement and restricted blood circulation.

The eyelets over the tendons and arch must be laced loosely. Just draw the lace up tightly enough to take in the slack leather and put enough tension on the lace so that it will not be drawn into the tighter sections around the ball of the foot and ankle. It's something you get the feel of after a while, by sensing when the lace is not tight enough to put pressure on the tendons and arch, and not loose enough to affect the lace tension above and below.

The top set of eyelets are crucial. These must be pulled tightly, gathering in all the loose leather around the ankle and heel, and drawing the foot firmly into the part of the skate that provides all the support. The boot's grasp in this area is what makes the skate an extension of the shin bone, enabling the skater to balance and perform other drills without difficulty.

This top set of eyelets must be pulled tightly, but again, tightly is a relative term. A pair of skates with rock-hard ankle support will need only a medium degree of tightness, enough not to interfere with circulation or tendon movement. *But once a skate's counters go soft, no amount of eye-popping pressure on those laces will restore support.*

I've seen hundreds of kids in absolute misery because they think or have been told that tight lacing will overcome any lack of support in their skates. Despite frozen feet and aching arches, they struggle gamely through drills and scrimmages, convinced that this is all part of the game. Their skate laces are so tight they actually twang like violin strings. The guts and determination it must take to stay at it is fantastic. Yet it's all so stupidly unnecessary.

Remember this—the top set of eyelets must be tight, but when they have to be tightened to a degree where they create discomfort, there is something wrong with the skates.

At this point, while lacing and tightening the last eyelets, there are two major mistakes made.

- Skipping the top eyelet. I shudder every time I see it, because the last eyelet is the most important one. Either through laziness or because it is tucked up under the shin pad overhang, too many boys do not bother with the top eyelet. Yet that is the key point to which all the extra leather is drawn to give complete support. Don't let any skater miss the last eyelet.

- Wrapping extra lengths of lace around the ankle or down under the arch of the skate. Most boys end up with adult-size laces in their skates, leaving 12 inches to 14 inches extra when they finish lacing. By now I should not have to tell you what happens when that lace is tied around the ankle or arch. Right. Additional pressure is placed on the Achilles tendon or arch, and the blood circulation is stopped.

Never, but never, tie a lace around the top of the skate or down under it. It's a bad habit that must be broken. Extra lengths of lace should be tied in a double or triple bow at the top eyelet, where they belong. And when tying the bow, loop the lace twice before forming the actual bow, to prevent slippage.

Finally, for people who are chafed by the tight lacing in the top three eyelets, a piece of half-inch thick foam rubber is the answer. Make it as wide as the skate tongue and place it beneath the tongue under the top three eyelets when lacing up. This relieves chafing, provides extra room for the ankle tendons to function, and will not detract from the supporting capacity of the boot.

The foam rubber precaution is a must at the start of the hockey season. Some peoples' tendons project more than others', and, if you restrict their movement, become severely bruised. Reminds me of a bone bruise, the kind I used to get on the palm of my hand early in the baseball season. There isn't any remedy for this, except long soaks in Epsom salts and warm water.

Care of the Blade

I get turned off every time I hear someone say a skate blade should be 'rockered' to give you better turning power or greater maneuverability. A *rockered blade* is one that is slightly rounded from toe to heel, like the rocker of a rocking chair. If the blade is placed on a very flat surface you can 'rock' the skate slightly from front to back.

I strongly disagree that this has any great advantage. The key to skating and playing hockey is the ability to develop power, and that starts with the contact of blade and ice. The more blade you have in contact with the ice, the better *purchase*, or *grip*, you will have when accelerating, which gives you more speed. Hence you can get away from a standing start much faster.

I don't think skates should be rockered any more than they are when they leave the manufacturer. When taking skates in for sharpening, tell the operator to follow the manufacturer's blade pattern and not to take any extra steel off the toe and heel. Tell him to grind off the same amount over the full length of the blade, and if necessary, stay there to make sure he does it. You are paying for a service and have every right to expect it to be performed the way you want it to be.

Too many skate sharpeners work for their own convenience, to handle as many skates as possible in the shortest period of time. Too often they act as if they are doing you a favour, and these are usually the guys who are not even qualified to sharpen an axe. A skate sharpener who takes pride in his skills will follow your directions, as long as he has not been brainwashed by the rocker crowd.

Most hockey players have their skates sharpened too often. Every time they get a small nick or burr on the blade edge they rush the skates in for resharpening. This is one of the main causes of unnecessary wear on the blade. The abrasion is usually caused by stepping on a nail head or on concrete, or locking skates with someone on the ice. The damage can be quickly repaired with a small, rectangular carborundum stone that sells for less than a buck. I consider it the most important piece of equipment in my (and my three sons') hockey bag.

The stone will not sharpen skates, but it takes off burrs and other build-ups of steel on each side of the damaged part. This restores the sharp edge on each side of the nick, and in all damage cases but the most severe, will not affect skating performance.

Run your thumb down the side of the blade and you will feel the nicks and burrs quite easily. Wet the stone, lay it flat, lengthwise along the side of the blade, and run it back and forth several times. By removing all the burrs this way you can save many unnecessary sharpenings and add years to the life of your blades.

Most arenas where I have been, have concrete floors between the dressing rooms and ice surface. Keep a sharp lookout too for nailheads in dressing room floors, hallways, stairs, players' boxes and penalty boxes. Believe it or not, I've

often seen as many as three nailheads sticking out one-quarter to one-half inch above the floor surface. If these don't get you, the steel pipe which acts as support for the boards in the players' benches will. How the architects can justify this lack of consideration for hockey players, I'll never know. One thing is certain—those talented gentlemen have never played a game of hockey in their lives!

If a player must walk on cement he should go flat-footed, not on his toes. Concentrating all the weight on the toe of the blade is certain to cause burrs or more severe damage. It is ironic that most people walk on their toes on concrete, because most people develop power from this part of their blade. That makes it doubly wrong for them to burr their toes. I develop power from the centre part of the blade, so if anyone should walk on their toes, I should. Walking flat-footed, without dragging the feet, gives the player a chance to reach the ice without ruining the blade edge.

But that is a last resort. Each player should carry scabbards or blade guards at all times, and wear them when crossing any hard surface like concrete. He can take them off at the bench, and wear them back to the dressing room. But once in the dressing room, the scabbards should be removed and the blades dried completely, because wet blades left in the scabbard for several days can cause severe rusting. I have seen blades rusted so badly that, when combined with poor sharpening, which strained the front edges of the blades, they actually cracked when put under a heavy strain on the ice.

Care of the Boot

I have had one pair of skates for about 20 years, and another pair 12 years. The 20-year-old pair now has its third set of blades and is in good enough shape to take a fourth set, except that the rivet holes in the bottom are so enlarged that I doubt the next set can be firmly anchored. The boots of both pair are in beautiful condition, thanks to a preservation method that some people have warned would make my skates fall apart. Well, if they do suddenly disintegrate now, it will still be worthwhile, for in recent years I have been using my skates about four times as often as I did in my busiest N.H.L. season.

I have been treating my skates with shellac since before my junior hockey days. At various times I have tried four or five different waterproofing materials, and have found nothing like clear shellac. It also makes an excellent protective material for toe caps.

I would recommend that new skates get at least six coats of clear shellac before they are used. Leather skates should be painted ankle high, with special emphasis on the seams, particularly where the boot toe meets the blade. Unless this aperture is filled with shellac, you'll get wet feet. If you have nylon skates, use a good silicone waterproofing. One word of caution—the leather should be completely dry before painting, or the shellac will turn a milky colour. And allow at least two to three hours between coats.

Shellacking is especially important for lower-priced skates, where continual exposure to moisture will eventually soften the counters. I know dozens of youngsters whose skates never dry out from beginning to end of a hockey season. You have probably seen the result yourself— the boots are as soft as kid gloves when wet, and brittle as glass when dry.

Shellac is also the best protective material I know for the toe caps of good-quality skates. After many coats of shellac, there is no way the toe caps will get any more than superficial damage from chips and cuts.

After the initial application, new skates should get regular treatment about once a month. There are countless coats of shellac on my 20-year-old skates (almost armour-plated!) and despite many battle scars, the leather is in such good shape that it will break my heart if I have to discard them.

I repeat, there have been warnings that shellac is harmful to skates, but in all my experience, I have never seen a boot that was damaged by this treatment.

The Hockey Stick

I have observed that the only way an

amateur or minor hockey league player does not imitate the professional is in his use of the stick. A pair of inadequate skates is a severe enough handicap for any boy, but an improper stick really tops it off. It says much for the determination of our youngsters that so many of them turn into good hockey players despite these handicaps. But where would these kids have gone if they had started out, shall we say, on the right skate?

Choosing a Stick

I recommend that you buy the best quality stick that is available, or that you can afford. A stick is too often purchased with the reasoning that "he will break it in a couple of games anyway, so why get a good one?" In the age group with which we are dealing, nine years to about 12 or 14 years, the percentage of broken sticks is very low. Most of them just splinter and fall apart, and with proper taping that can be avoided.

Most manufacturers do make a good quality, well-balanced stick for boys, but they are not always available in every part of the country. The retailer must take his share of the blame for this, because he also thinks—and recommends—that a cheap or adult sized stick is all the kids need.

If you can find a retailer that handles a quality stick for boys, let the youngster choose one for himself, but use the following guidelines on *lie* and blade curve.

Stick Lie

The lie of a stick is the angle when looking at it from the side—between the handle and the ice. It is indicated by a number on the top side of the stick near the end of the handle. The lie is graduated from number four to number seven. (5)

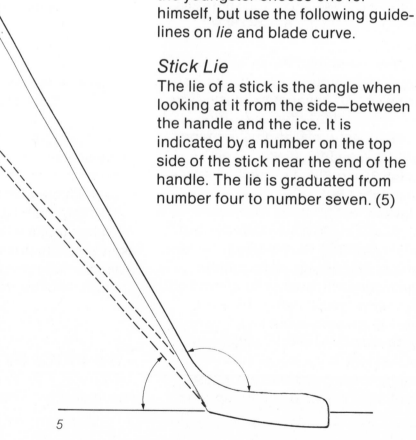

Lie 7

Lie 4

5

When the bottom of the stick blade is flat on the ice, the handle end of a lie four is much closer to the ice than the lie seven. Another way of putting it is that the lower number indicates a higher angle between the handle and blade, the higher number, a lower angle.

I think that until a boy becomes a proficient stickhandler he should use the highest possible lie and a blade with a straight edge on the bottom from heel to toe. If you purchase by lie number, you are going to run into the same problem as with skate sizes—the angle of a lie five, for example, will differ from one manufacturer to another. One of these years the hockey stick industry will get around to a standard lie but until then, when buying a boy's stick, I recommend you find the highest lie possible and then buy the best quality stick in that line.

Why the high lie? Most youngsters are quite weak in the hands, wrists, arms and shoulders. These parts of the anatomy are not strong enough at their stage of development to provide the muscle power necessary to learn new skills in stickhandling. Using a high lie stick enables a player to bring the puck in closer to his feet where he can apply what strength he has to the business end of it. It also nearly forces the boy into the proper stickhandling and skating positions. In my opinion a high lie stick is a tremendous advantage to boys in the age group with which we are concerned.

Again, until the boy has mastered the basics of stickhandling and passing, I think he should use a straight or 'centre' blade, not one that is curved for left or right hand shooting. You should also stay away from blades with curved or rockered bottom edges until the boy is old and experienced enough to determine if these special blades are of any advantage to him,

At this point you have chosen either a properly designed boy's stick, or have had to settle for an adult stick to get good quality. I am often asked "What is the best stick on the market for a boy?" Well, there are so many on the market, along with the number sold on just a regional basis, that I really don't know. All I can suggest is: find the manufacturer that makes the highest lie, and buy the best stick in that line. It has been my experience that some manufacturers of boys' sticks put an adult sized handle on a small blade in their top line of youths' sticks. This is a serious handicap. The handle, which is too thick for small hands to grip, is so stiff and over-sized it lacks personality—no feel, no flexibility.

Why should I expect my 12-year-old to play hockey, carrying the puck with a stick built for adult hands? He can't feel the puck when he's carrying it!

What we need is a high quality stick with personality, balance and feel—and the manufacturer who makes it won't be able to supply the demand. Two of my sons used experimental models this past summer—medium size blades, three-quarter size handles, light with feel, stiff yet flexible when necessary, and durable. They used them two and one-half hours daily for ten weeks. These sticks are the best of the hundreds I've seen this past summer. The manufacturer has a winner.

You may end up with an adult stick in order to get the best combination of quality and lie.

Stick Length

The stick, the next most important piece of equipment after the skates, is subject to one major mistake by parents and boys. This is one instance where the youngsters fail in most cases to copy the pros. The kids' sticks are too long.

Years ago some well-meaning character came up with a formula for determining stick length: with skates on, stand the stick on its end in front of you and cut it off at chin level. The stick will be from two to four inches too long.

Next time you watch a professional hockey game from Montreal, look out for players who, during the playing of the National Anthem, stand their sticks in front of them. See where the top of the stick is— chest high, not chin high. Some time during their careers, they learned that the shorter stick is obviously better. Yet thousands of kids are starting out with the old nose or chin measurement. We sure don't make things easy for them, do we?

Here is what happens with a chin,

mouth, or nose-measured stick, one that is several inches too long. Stand the player with his feet 18 inches apart on the ice. With his hands in the normal position (the top hand grasping the stick at the end) have him place the blade on the ice. In order for him to get the full length of the blade on the ice, it will be necessary to draw his top hand back against his hip. In extreme cases, his top hand could be six to nine inches behind the body and as high as the waist or lower chest area. (6)

6

Standing still, it will be almost impossible for him to shoot or receive the puck or stickhandle without moving that top hand out in front of the body. In order to carry out these functions, the top hand will have to be well in front of the body, where it can be moved from side to side. As soon as the player does this, the toe, or front end of the blade, will lift several inches off the ice. Of course the player can overcome this by sliding both hands about six inches down the shaft of the stick and drawing the blade in closer to his feet. But he's sure going to look funny spearing himself with that six inches of butt end sticking out behind his top glove, every time he maneuvers the stick in front of his stomach.

If you think he feels awkward standing still, try to visualize what happens when he starts skating.

When a player starts to move, he must automatically crouch lower in order to utilize his hip and leg power. Naturally, the lower he goes, the higher the toe of his stick lifts off the ice. Then, in order to bring the blade of his stick flush with the ice again, he has to slide both hands even further down the shaft.

Thousands of hockey coaches must have seen the result—a kid stickhandling down the ice with anywhere from two inches to five inches of the handle jutting out behind his top hand! The observant coach, or the rare one who really knows his hockey basics, should immediately realize that the boy's stick is too long.

In (7), the boy's stick is the correct length. With blade flat on the ice, both hands are free to pass in front of the body, the body is erect with eyes looking ahead, and the boy can maintain the position without danger of getting a sore back.

Here (8) the boy is standing, with top hand indicating where the stick should be cut off. Note the amount

7

8

of stick behind the hand. It makes a hell of a weapon for spearing yourself!

The passing position shown here, (9), would be impossible if that extra piece of stick was spearing the boy. The top hand would not be free to move in front of the body as it does here.

Here you see demonstrated the tangible difference. (10) One stick is

9

10

Then try the same thing yourself, or have a boy try it, with a stick that is measured to his chin or nose. See what I mean?

In order for the vast majority of boys to stickhandle, pass and shoot properly, the end of their sticks (when stood on end in the traditional manner) should come no higher than the top of their chests.

That's the only way the pro can dipsy-doodle the puck—by passing both hands back and forth in front of his body—and still keep the blade of his stick flat on the ice. Chances are you could not identify his stick (by length) when stood in a rack with a team of Bantams' sticks.

Learn this well. After poor skates, a stick that is too long is the next most outrageous handicap we can give a young player.

Trimming the Stick
Many people are forced to buy an adult stick for their youngsters in order to get the good quality. Their problem is not solved simply by cutting it off to the right length. This creates a completely unbalanced stick, with a short handle and a vastly oversized blade. It has no feel, no life, no 'personality' of its own. A fast pass taken on the end of the blade will probably twist the stick out of the boy's hands.

The solution may seem like a lot of trouble, but if you are going to buy a good stick, why go halfway? You must trim the blade down to the right proportion.

If you can, before leaving the

chin length. That's the one that caused all the trouble in (6). The other stick, used in (7), (9), is chest high.

Next time you see an N.H.L. game on television, take your eyes off the puck for a change and examine the man who is carrying the puck. In nearly all cases, when stickhandling, *both hands are in front of the body*.

sporting goods store, place a youth-sized blade against the side of your adult blade, and trace the smaller outline with pen or pencil. Just make sure the heels and bottom of the two blades are lined up, and you will have the right pattern to follow. Then you can use a coping saw, jig saw, or anything you can lay your hands on, to trim the big blade down to its proper proportion. Sandpaper the rough edges, put several coats of shellac on the raw wood (and the rest of the blade while you're at it) and presto—a great little stick.

Don't worry if you cannot find a blade pattern to follow. You can take up to an inch and a half off the length of the blade, and up to one-half inch off the height, without doing any serious damage. In fact, I have seen many youngsters whose fathers hacked far too much off the blade length and it didn't seem to bother their puck handling at all. Or watch the kids playing street hockey with only three or four inches of blade left on their sticks—does it appear to be a handicap?

Taping the Stick

A good hockey stick, unless it has a built-in flaw, should last the average boy three to four months with proper taping. My own boys play as much hockey as most and the one who tapes his stick well, uses two, maybe three sticks a year. The other one hardly bothers with tape and he manages to go through ten or 12. It's not hard to see that the 'old man' buys the sticks in this family!

Kids up to 12 years old are normally not strong enough to break a well-made stick, unless their coach lets them get slap-shot happy. What usually happens is that water gets into the joints where the stick is laminated, and it splits or slowly disintegrates. Taping the stick, particularly in the heel area, protects the varnish that keeps the blade waterproof. Once the varnish wears off the bottom of a stick, its lifetime is limited.

I have found after years of experimenting with every kind of tape available, that the plastic electrical tape is by far the best. Most other tapes, particularly the old friction tape we once used, wear through in one practice or game. Black plastic tape lasts twice, sometimes three times as long.

Start taping the stick at the toe, right next to the end of the blade, and, overlapping about half the width of the tape, work toward the heel. Go past the heel and then work back over the heel again and maybe one-quarter way up the blade. This will give you two layers of tape on the ice. By replacing the top layer when it wears through, you will always have one layer of tape protecting the heel of the stick.

At one time, I was one of a great many players who believed that taping a stick didn't make much difference in its lifetime; besides, with the Toronto Maple Leafs picking up the tab, who cared if a few extra sticks were broken? But you learn quickly when working with several thousand kids, and paying a few bills yourself, that taking the little extra time and trouble with a stick is well worth it. I know of very few youngsters and even fewer minor hockey teams who can afford to go around beating hockey sticks into matchsticks.

It's time the manufacturers, who know very well how to extend the life of their product, stop treating the item as expendable and start including a few simple instructions with hockey sticks.

2
Protective Equipment

Equipment manufactured for the professional and adult hockey player is generally excellent and gives great protection. But hockey equipment for boys can generally be classified as junk. It's difficult to put the blame on anyone in particular, because manufacturers are responding to a demand for cheaper equipment for kids. Parents are reluctant to buy expensive gear that will be outgrown in a couple of years. I can't understand why. Money should be no object in this game. If a kid's going into an aggressive sport, he needs the protection. If he doesn't have that protection, he shouldn't be playing. Still parents insist on cheap stuff, and hope their child can get to be a star without coming in violent contact with the boards, ice surface, goal posts, hockey sticks, skates, pucks, other players (and their fists) and the occasional missile from the stands. Some hope.

The most you can say for boys' hockey equipment is that it looks good. But if you examine it closely, you will see that foam rubber is substituted for shock absorbing padding. Foam rubber is useless for absorbing impact. Vital areas, especially around flexible joints in the body, are left unprotected simply because it costs too much to build in the protection.

The manufacturer can make his boys' equipment look professional, but in no way can you depend on the phrase "what you see is what you get."

Do It Yourself Safety

What can be done? You'll be surprised to know that what you do get for under $13.95 can be turned into very good equipment, at relatively little expense, by adding your own protection.

The best shock absorber available today is a material called *ensolite*. This is the manufacturer's name. It is also known as *Rubb-o-tex*, and in the trade, as *310V*. It's used in gymnasium mats and most high-priced hockey equipment, and looks something like compacted foam rubber. But where foam rubber just fills space, one-quarter to one-half inch of ensolite will take most of the sting out of almost any impact received on the ice.

Most goal tenders' shoulder pads are lined with ensolite, or have pockets where the padding can be inserted. Ask your local sporting goods dealer if he has ensolite inserts and purchase several sets, or enough to modify what hockey equipment you have.

You may have to really scout around because ensolite is not commercially available in its natural form. Enough questions to your sports store proprietor will get you on the track of the manufacturer, from whom you can order it.

Gloves
We'll start at the scene of one of the biggest acts of criminal negligence. You can be pretty sure that most hockey gloves sold at under $20

leave the wearer wide open for injury. They can give excellent protection on the back of the hand, the fingers and thumb. But in all lower-priced gloves—and I mean all—there is no protection for the most vital area, the wrist.

Most gloves have one piece of fibre that protects the thumb, and another over the top of the wrist. If you examine a boy's glove you will see a gap wide enough to admit a blow from a hockey stick between the two fibres, on the inside of the wrist. (11) Now this won't make

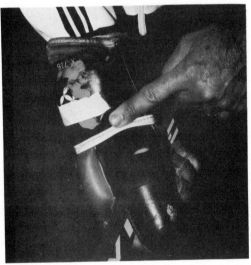

11

much difference for the hand on the upper end of the stick which, when it does receive a blow, usually takes it on the back of the hand and wrist. But the lower hand, which is wrist up when in position, takes a real pounding from opposing players' sticks. If you have a youngster, put on his gloves and look at the position of his hands on the stick; you will see what

I mean. The upper hand is against the body with padding facing outward; the lower hand has the padding facing downward, vulnerable to attack from above. That attack, from a well-swung stick, can be devastating.

Another weak spot in many gloves is fibre not backed by padding. A piece of hard fibre can feel substantial, but just try laying a piece of it over your hand or wrist and whacking it with a stick. It hurts like hell, unless there is some shock absorber under it.

Defects in manufacturers' gloves will vary from one brand to another, but they are not hard to spot if you know what to look for . . . foam rubber padding and unprotected gaps on the wrist between the two pieces of padding. Don't despair, reach for the ensolite.

Cut a piece of the material just big enough to cover the unprotected area and glue it in the appropriate place inside the glove. (12) Ask your

12

shoemaker to recommend a glue.

Remember, the two key places to watch are at the base of the thumb, and inside the wrist on the glove hand lower on the stick (the right glove for right-hand shots, the left glove for left handers). You don't have to bother with the glove on the upper hand, it seldom moves far enough away from the body to leave its soft underside exposed. A small piece of additional shock-absorbing material will improve most boys' gloves to the point where they offer as good protection as that received by the pros.

There are two more things to watch for when buying boys' gloves. One of the most important senses in developing a boy's puck handling ability is 'feeling' the position of the puck on the stick blade. The player's hands must become his eyes. To get this feel, the glove's palm leather should be reasonably thin, pliable and tough. This grade of leather is probably too expensive for boys' gloves, but it doesn't hurt to look for it. I know that the gloves worn by most boys in my hockey schools are so insensitive to feel that I make them practise puck handling with bare hands on the stick. Boys' gloves should fit—just as skates do. The other point to remember? Don't buy them too big.

Helmet

No boy in any of my hockey schools dares to step on the ice without wearing a helmet. And if I had my way, every hockey player in the country, regardless of age, would be forced to wear a helmet when performing. Parents should make sure their youngsters become accustomed to wearing a helmet from the first time they step on the ice. They're the most sensible and necessary pieces of protection there are, and big league players who refuse to wear them for 'cosmetic' reasons are not only stupid, they're selfish.

Most helmets available for young players today provide adequate protection. But buy only those that have the C.S.A. (Canadian Standards Association) seal of approval. The only other point for a coach to watch is that the chin strap is buckled at all times.

Shoulder Pads

Shoulder pads that prepare a boy for action in the Canadian Football League are a bit much. Many kids are over-equipped for minor league hockey, actually burdened down with unnecessary gear. Some shoulder pads carry far too much protection where it isn't necessary, and typically, don't have enough where it's needed most.

Firstly, I don't think kids need the protection that many pads give them over the top of the chest and over the shoulder blades in the back. Try to avoid pads that have heavy fibre plates in these areas.

Secondly, look for pads that have good shock-absorbing material over the upper arm and biceps area. This is where many pieces of shoulder equipment are sadly lacking.

All that's necessary for the actual shoulder area is a fibre cap backed up by a good shock absorber. Most pads provide this to a reasonably good degree. Most of the kids in my leagues get good protection from the fibre caps that hook on their braces. But, as I mentioned, they need something more than foam rubber or some other cheap substitute over the upper arm and biceps when the high sticking, slashing and cross checking starts.

Once again, get out the ensolite, cut a piece to fit over the biceps and outer arm, and glue it in place. This turns a six dollar set of shoulder pads into something approaching a $25 pair for protection purposes.

Elbow Pads

If I had to play a game with only one piece of protective equipment, I would choose elbow pads. Broken fingers, bad cuts, severe bruises will mend, but with a screwed-up elbow—you're in trouble.

An elbow pad with a good heavy fibre cap backed up with a shock-absorbing material provides adequate protection for the tip of the elbow. Don't buy pads, even for the smallest kids, without that fibre cap.

But once again, when you consider that the arms take more punishment than any other part of the body, I think the elbow pad should do something more than protect one key spot. If shoulder pads can be modified to protect the upper arm, elbow pads can also be

fixed to cover the lower, or forearm. I recommend that a piece of ensolite be fastened to the lower band of the elbow pad to extend protection down to the top of the glove gauntlet. Remember, under normal conditions only the outer part of the arm takes the punishment, so don't get carried away with excess padding.

Shin Pads

Here is another example of boys' equipment looking like the professional stuff while giving about as much protection as spats on a sparrow.

First of all, when purchasing, drive the retailer round the bend until he can tell you whether the sewing on the pad is chain stitched or not. Shin pads are particularly vulnerable to skate cuts and when a chain stitch is severed, the whole pad can be unzipped in seconds just by pulling on the thread. (13) Any manufacturer who uses a chain stitch on any hockey equipment, should be

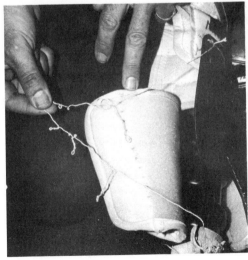

13

dragged over the arctic ice pack on his bare corporate keester.

Once you are sure the pad will stay together for a reasonable length of time, worry about the padding. Most of today's pads depend on an air pocket or spacer to protect the shin bone from impact. The hard fibre or plastic outer shell, is usually substantial enough for minor league play, provided the supporting straps keep it well clear of the shin bone.

But if the knee cap is protected in the same way–that is, without shock-absorbing material between the plastic cap and the skin–then the pad can be dangerous. And you would be amazed at how many kids' knee pads are made without padding under the knee cap. Yet one hard shot, taken on the fibre pad next to the skin, could shatter it. The answer, of course, is the installation of a good shock-absorbing material behind the knee pad.

Look at (14). See the space between the knee cap and shin pad.

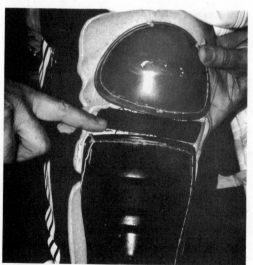

14

Believe it or not, this area has no protection, although it's one of the most sensitive areas on the leg. To remedy the problem, cut a strip of ensolite and paste it inside the shin pad over this area.

There is one other danger that kids are exposed to because of careless equipment shopping. Shin pads that are too long will ride up the leg so that the fibre knee cap is actually several inches above the knee. This puts the flexible portion between the two hard fibre caps directly over the knee, and is another invitation to disaster. This flexible portion is usually made of very poor protective material, and a shot hitting it *hurts*. Pay special attention to this area and reinforce it.

You must resist the temptation to buy oversized adult shin pads for your youngster, on the premise that he'd have better protection. Buy pads that fit, and then add the extra protection if necessary. You will end up with equipment as good, with a saving of ten or fifteen dollars.

One more thing on the subject of the proper wearing of shin pads. I saw a young fellow fall on one knee during hockey drills recently and wondered why he rolled around in pain. It turned out he was depending on tight hockey stockings to hold his shin pads in place. They didn't—and when he fell, the knee pad slipped off to one side. He was lucky he didn't suffer permanent damage, and learned the hard way to wear garters over the pads.

Pants

Every young hockey player gets his first good look at the ceiling of an arena from flat on his back or the seat of his pants. One would imagine that the buttocks at least would be protected, but it's not so.

The standard padding in lower-priced hockey pants is a piece of foam rubber that completely encircles the body. You should know by now the value of foam rubber. It looks good, but that's all. From my experience with minor hockey players, there are only three areas in this part of the body that need protection . . . the tailbone or base of the spine, the kidneys and the upper thigh.

Thousands of kids suffer painful injuries to the tailbone every year from the simple and natural act of falling on their keesters. Besides the hard ice surface, in many arenas there is a kick board that runs along the ice surface at the base of the boards. The kick board can protrude up to an inch, and there's hardly a game goes by without one or more kids falling from a scuffle along the boards right onto the kick board, tail first. Mister, that smarts. A boy can also be painfully injured by falling on a hockey stick, or sliding into a goal post. Come to think of it, every time I think I've seen the ultimate in strange accidents on the ice, the kids come up with a new twist.

You will find that most boys' hockey pants will need extra padding over the tailbone of the spine, and this can be added quite easily.

Fortunately, there are not many serious kidney injuries among kids in minor hockey but I've always felt it better to be safe than sorry. Consequently, I think parents should make sure that pants give adequate protection in the back area beneath the rib cage. A piece of ensolite can easily be installed in this area.

The charlie horse pads protect the upper thigh area—make sure these pads are backed with ensolite. When I played professional hockey, we wore pants that made at least an attempt at fitting properly. But what I see on boys today I just don't want to believe. When the hockey team buys the pants, the quality is good, but the man who does the ordering usually gets six large, eight medium and four small pair—he's lucky if six of the 18 pair fit well.

One place they will not fit is in the upper thigh area. The charlie horse pads can slide around, six to nine inches out of place—anywhere but where they're most needed for protection.

When I began to buy my own equipment, I attached a strip of three inch wide elastic to both sides of the charlie horse pockets inside the pants. I slipped my leg through this loop—and the pad stayed in position, regardless of my position.

Jockstrap and Cup

At a hockey school recently I saw an eight-year-old with a big lump on his hip. Thinking it to be an apple or orange tucked away for an emergency snack I slapped it with my stick and said "hey Tommy, what's that?"

"My jockstrap", he said.

He was wearing combination pants and stockings—like woolen pantihose—with a built-in jockstrap and protective cup supported by snap-in tapes. It was like trying to keep a ten-gallon hat over an apple in a windstorm.

All kids should wear an athletic supporter or a snug pair of jockey shorts underneath the protective cup, but everything should fit, because if a cup starts wandering around the groin area, it sets up another dangerous situation. When a player becomes overheated, the testicles sag further away from the body. They have a built-in thermostat. When cold, they snuggle up close; when warm, they try to get away from the source of heat.

Unsupported testicles can stray outside the protective cup, and when the opposite edge of that cup receives a blow . . . well, anyone whose foot has slipped off the pedal while standing up pumping a bicycle will know what I mean.

Most children's hockey equipment, because of cost limitations, does not provide adequate protection for the kids who wear it. But it does provide a framework on which you can build all the protection your child will need. Don't go overboard out of concern for their safety; kids are a lot tougher than we think.

But do examine his equipment closely; common sense will tell you where it is deficient. The points I have covered are the main ones, but if your child is a defenceman who likes to step in front of slap shots, you can either protect him, or talk a little sense into him.

3
The Art
of Skating

Balance and Power

If you don't think skating can be an art, just watch a figure skater. Skating in a hockey game requires just as much skill and finesse, but hockey players don't particularly care about looking graceful when they perform. The incredible sense of balance required by figure skating is also the key requirement for a hockey player—he can't develop power without it.

Learning Balance

The ability to balance and develop power must be taught by using the correct skating posture. You can't do it by standing up straight; the proper position is a slight semicrouch with knees bent slightly, shoulders over the knees and knees over the ball of the foot. (15)

In (16), the boy is in the correct front position for skating, with head

16

up, body in a semicrouch, and the supporting leg directly underneath him and slightly bent, while the right leg pushes out to develop power.

It's funny, but the first time kids try to adopt this position on the ice, they fall down. Yet they get into the same position almost every day, when they go into the bathroom, crouch slightly and drop their pants.

The problem when crouching on skates is the tendency to balance on the toe or heel. The result is a youngster sprawling on the ice. The skill to be learned is balancing flat-footed on the centre portion of the blade because that section is crucial to all the skating skills that follow. One of the first steps in teaching the right posture is getting a boy on skates to squat down on his heels with feet shoulder width apart, arms extended forward, and head tilted up, facing ahead. In this position he has to balance on the flat of his

15

blades or he will fall.

Now you should notice that his body symmetry follows a certain pattern: the shoulders, knees and balls of the feet are in a vertical line. The moment this symmetry is broken, the boy is off balance and falls.

When the boy rises from the squat and begins to skate, the same pattern holds true. The leg that supports the body weight during a stride will be lined up with a shoulder. As the weight transfers from leg to leg, the body symmetry will always follow: shoulder over the knee, knee over the ball of the foot. This is difficult to explain to a boy, but he learns it instinctively. However, it's useful information for coaches when diagnosing skating problems.

Through balance exercises, skating sessions should teach a boy to develop the power and strength he already has in his legs. A boy can't develop this natural power unless he has mastered balance. Only then should leg strengthening exercises begin.

Developing Power

Power or thrust is created by a skate blade describing a semicircle on the ice. If the body is not properly balanced on the supporting leg, the driving leg must disengage from the ice before it has completed its full cycle of developing power, or the player falls on his face.

The amount of power developed by the thrusting skate can easily be read on clean ice. Send skaters onto a freshly flooded ice surface one at a time, and have them skate full out between the blue lines. The degree of curve in the skate cuts will indicate the amount of power developed. A sharp curve that ends more than 45 degrees from the skater's direction shows close to maximum thrust. A very slight curve in the skate cut indicates low power, because the skater had to transfer weight off the driving leg prematurely to maintain his balance.

In order to develop full power, a skater must therefore have the ability to turn his toes outward. That's when his skate is really biting the ice and giving him push.

When skating backward, the reverse is true. From a standing start, the skater must turn the toe of one skate in toward the other, transfer weight to the turned foot and start pushing backward. Power is developed as the blade describes a semicircle to the rear. Weight is then transferred to the other leg, which points toe inward and cuts another semicircle to the rear.

The ability to turn the toes inward and outward is fundamental to good skating, yet is an extremely difficult exercise for kids to perform. I have found that most youngsters have locked hips, which results from having performed all walking and running movements in one direction only—straight ahead. The hips, knees, ankles and feet are just not flexible enough to allow the leg to go through a full power cycle on skates.

This is what causes the youngster to start losing his balance, just when the toe of his thrusting foot is turning outward for its maximum push. He has no choice but to disengage the skate before he falls.

One of the first jobs that must be done with a boy is to unlock his hips, and that includes all the joints from there down. Unless this is done, the upper half of the body goes through some wild contortions in order to let the lower half perform. This is the first habit a coach must break— using the head, arms and shoulders to skate.

Remember this: A hockey player skates from his hips down, and plays hockey from his hips up.

I think the ideal hockey skater should have ball-bearing joints in the lower half of his body, like a Hawaiian belly dancer. But first we'll look at a different example.

Most of you have watched speed skaters perform. When breaking out from the starting line, they need every ounce of strength and leverage they can muster to dig their extra-long blades into the ice. With upper bodies bent almost horizontally, their extended arms swing in huge arcs from side to side with each stride. When developing power, they use every part of the body from head down for more leverage on their skates.

Once maximum speed is reached, the arms are tucked up behind the back and the skater maintains his momentum by hip and leg action alone. But for that extra spurt approaching the finish line, out come the arms again, and the whole body gets into the act.

Well, the hockey player doesn't have the luxury of getting his whole body into the act of skating. When he breaks out he is either carrying the puck or expecting to receive it, so his stick must be on the ice. The moment he begins wildly swinging his arms and shoulders to get more power, he's out of the hockey game.

Now let's dwell for a moment on the Hawaiian dancer. When performing, the upper body is almost motionless while the hands and arms apparently tell a story. But in the meantime, what those hips and legs are doing is something else. I have sometimes wondered what a coach could do with those dancers if they learned to skate from the hips down and play hockey from the hips up. It boggles the imagination.

The coach who balks at teaching belly dancing has to find some other way to get ball bearings into his players' hips. Believe me, it isn't easy, but it has to be done. The very first drills a boy must learn are designed to develop balance and flexibility.

As the player masters the balancing and unlocking drills he learns to get the maximum amount of skate blade on the ice and quickly becomes a better skater. He stops skating on his toes to prevent a forward fall, or on his heels to avoid a pratfall. When properly balanced, a skater's weight is on the centre portion of the blades where he gets the most purchase, or grip, on the ice.

The Rockered Blade Curse

But here is where you run into a serious problem—rockered blades. As we said earlier, most parents and children have been brainwashed into thinking that rockered skate blades are a must for any hockey player. That's pure hogwash, particularly as it applies to children. A rockered blade can have as little as one-half inch of steel on the ice, while an unmodified blade can put up to three or four inches of steel into action. What does that mean?

In (17), the skate blade is perfectly proportioned for maximum power development and sustained speed. The dotted line shows the amount of butchering some sharpeners will do to get what they consider is a properly rockered blade. It isn't, it's ridiculous.

Just imagine two high-powered dragsters lined up at the starting gate on a drag strip. Both cars are identical, except that one has tires a foot wide on the back wheels while the other is equipped with bicycle tires. The *GO* light flashes, both drivers hit the throttle and the cars are off in a cloud of smoke. You know who is going to win. The guy with the massive grip on the pavement will hit the finish line before old 'bicycle tires' goes a car length.

The same principle applies to skating. Kids whose skates have the biggest bite on the ice will develop far more power and speed than boys whose rockered blades barely scratch the surface.

Think of the speed skater. His extra long blades give him fantastic purchase on the ice when accelerating, but more importantly, he can sustain his speed for miles and miles. With all that blade transmitting his leg power to the ice, he requires much less physical effort, maintaining top speed with long, slow strides.

Though speed skates are impractical for hockey, because its impossible to maneuver quickly on them, don't forget the relation of purchase to power and speed. When a youngster adds good balance and posture, he is headed in the right direction.

Practice Philosophy

One of the questions I am asked most often is "when should my kid start learning hockey?"

My answer has to be tailored to the boy, and local conditions—meaning the availability of ice time. For example, I'm against using ice time for six to eight-year-olds and

17

even for excellent teen-aged hockey players, at the expense of teenage recreational hockey. A teenager who is only an average player can't get near the ice for a fun game in many communities, while all the very best teenagers are playing regularly.

If you have the luxury of adequate ice time for all the 16 to 18-year-olds who want to play hockey, and still have ice availability, by all means start the small fry.

Normally around the ninth year is a good time to start teaching the game. From nine to 12 years of age the practice time should be spent mainly on fundamentals, not game tactics or philosophy. They should concentrate on skating, puck handling and passing.

I have a peewee system of 24 teams playing recreational hockey once a week. When one boy begins to dominate or stand out on his team, we put him in one of six competitive teams. Then we have one more club—call them the Mini-Stars—formed from the best of these six competitive teams.

After Christmas, one-quarter of the Mini-Stars' practice time is devoted to game philosophy—situations such as getting the puck out of their own end, killing penalties, winning face-offs, etc. But the other 45 minutes are still used for skill fundamentals. Now these kids are pretty good, the best of 30 teams in the system, but I know they still need constant puck handling and passing drills. The other 30 teams get no game philosophy, only the basics. I think this is the only way to ensure that eventually we will have all kinds of talent in the 16 to 18 year age group.

I feel the little kids should develop game sense through common sense: let them make all the tactical mistakes they want, as long as they have a ball. They'll also win their share of games just by being pretty good skaters and passers; the rest, you might say, comes naturally. They will develop to a considerable degree on their own, and be ready for game philosophy by the time they reach the 14 to 16 year age group.

I'll bet a lot of you are thinking that kids will not show up at non-competitive practices. Don't believe it. We run into some flak from parents, particularly those who come in from other parts of Canada and whose boys have literally been running the practices back home. In some cases, groups of parents will exert so much pressure on the coach that he will run the kind of practice the boys want, just to keep peace.

Well, we run the kind of practice we want, one we know is best for the boys. If the parents or boys don't like it, they are free to leave the scene. But once our philosophy is established, we get tremendous co-operation from everybody in the organization. We get 28 or 29 boys out of 30 showing up for a 7 a.m. practice.

I can anticipate your next problem as well. You have a team that plays once a week and gets a practice about every ten days. You live in a community that demands a winning team, no matter what the age. How do you concentrate on game fundamentals and still solve the immediate problem of winning every game?

The problem of increasing your practice time is simple to solve. Why shouldn't one coach get together with another to teach the basics? Instead of one practice per team every ten days, both teams can have two practices. And as every drill in this book is designed for 32 players, and four goal tenders, a dedicated coach can hardly turn down such an opportunity to utilize the drills fully.

As to the 'winning complex', you've got a problem, buddy. Your most difficult job will be convincing hockey authorities, parents and kids that they need a little patience. Tell them you can improve the skating ability of *every* boy on the club by 50% in one season, by following a pattern of basic drills for one-half of each practice period. That's all you want, just 30 minutes of every hour for fundamentals. You can practise game conditions for the remaining half hour. Then, as soon as the boys become better skaters, their puck handling and passing improve automatically. They become better all-round hockey players.

When you get into the skating drills, your next reaction will be "how in hell can I teach that when I can't even do it myself?" I've heard it dozens of times and the answer is simple. You don't have to demonstrate it, not as long as you have some kids who are not afflicted with pot bellies, smoker's lungs and flabby muscles.

The coach should read the drills thoroughly before the practice and make sure he understands, in theory, what has to be done. Then in the dressing room he can explain the drills to the kids and demonstrate in street shoes. Next let them try it on the ice. Several kids will pick it up right away, and these will become your ice demonstrators. All the coach must do is be able to recognize the right and wrong way of performing the drills and correct any mistakes.

Get the three or four players who learn each drill or skill quickly, and have them work with your three or four slowest learners. Personal attention to each boy is a must, but its impossible for the coach to spend more than a minute or so with each boy and also supervise a group. Your fast learners will enjoy helping the slower ones, and you can concentrate on the group of average players.

There's one thing I insist upon when youngsters are practising the drills. No one is allowed to have both hands on the stick. A kid hasn't mastered body control yet, and when skating with a stick held in both hands, swings it back and forth like a high speed scythe. Somebody skating beside him will get a mouth or eye full of blade for sure. It's something you constantly have to remind them of, because they forget the rule instantly.

If you're a coach, you must have concern for the kids' safety, so make them skate with just the top hand on the stick, and the blade on the ice at all times. If you can't enforce that rule, then turn in your whistle.

The coach has to be a great motivator. He has to make the practice as much fun as a game, and it can be done. He's got to growl and praise when necessary. He should never spend so long at one drill that it becomes too tiring or boring, and he should utilize certain boys to help make his job easier.

When working with many groups of boys, I find it a great psychological tool to put the boys' names on their helmets, with wide masking tape, last name on the front and first name on the back. When supervising drills, I stand in front of them correcting and commenting as they come toward me. Usually I'm growling something like "get your backside down, Smith," and poor Smith has me on his back until he finally gets it.

Then, when he skates past doing the drill properly, I turn around and holler "hey Jimmy!" When he looks back I say "hey, that was real good. Way to go." The look of pleasure on his face is something to see. I use the boys' last names when correcting or chastising, first names when praising.

Before starting the drills you must establish the speed at which they must be performed. It's not a race, although the boys are tempted to go fast because the balance drills are easier at high speed. But they must be made to take their time, doing the drills at slow to medium speed. They

have to be able to master the drills at slow speeds or most of the value of the exercise is lost.

Use of Pylons

The use of pylons is very important, but unless they are placed properly, forget it. Without them to mark out the skating course, it's almost impossible to control a bunch of kids. No matter how many times you explain where they are to skate, they will end up going all over the place and your drills will collapse in confusion. It's necessary to use the whole rink surface, not just two-thirds of it.

For skating drills, place pylons on the four face-off spots inside the end zones, or even slightly deeper if you wish, and four more on the blue lines on each side of the rink. (Widen the teaching area for large groups.) The boys skate around the ice outside of the pylons, and perform the drills between the blue lines on each side. The pylons at the blue lines remind them where to start and stop the drill.

If your club doesn't have pylons, you'll have to scrounge a couple of dozen from the local department of highways or get a merchant to donate them.

I cannot place too much importance on the proper use of pylons during the skating and other drills to follow. They must be carefully positioned each time out on the ice to make the team utilize every available inch of ice. The coach and instructors must jump on any player who starts taking short cuts or ignores the course marked out by

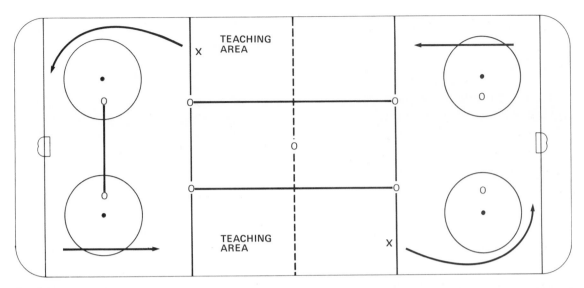

O   Pylons
X   Instructors
➞ Direction of course

18

pylons. When using the blue line to blue line performance area, it is vital for the player to begin the drill as soon as he hits the starting blue line. When he takes a short cut through the end zone, he cannot be ready in time and most of your prime instruction time is lost.

Skating Drills

Drill 1–Squat

Set up the course pylons. (18) Holding the top hand on the stick, skate toward the blue line at slow to medium speed. On approaching the blue line, start gliding on both feet, with feet approximately shoulder width apart. When you reach the blue line, sit down on both heels with both arms extended forward, back straight and shoulders over the

19

knees. (19) Most boys fall when first trying this drill, but keep reminding them to hold their heads forward as it has quite an effect on their centre of gravity. Check the width of the

20

21

22

23

feet as they have a tendency to go too far apart or too close together. (See (20) for correct position, and (21) (22) for legs too far apart, legs too close together.) The stick, as in all skating drills, is on the ice pointing forward, held by the top hand.

When they have settled into the

squat and are fully balanced, they then lift one foot off the ice and extend the leg in front of them, keeping the skate *off the ice.* (23) Now they are balanced on one leg. They hold this position until they reach the second blue line, then stand up and skate away, doing the same drill on the opposite side of the ice.

During the squat, make sure the boys' seats are right down on their heels. Place one instructor on each blue line to supervise and check the boys' performance. This drill will give you some idea of how bad most boys' sense of balance really is. But keep them at it for only five minutes at the most each time, and in no time the whole team will be able to zip right through it.

The importance of good skates will also become obvious during this drill. A boy who goes over on his ankles from lack of support will find it almost impossible to perform. And when he has to balance his whole weight on one skate, there's no way he can remain upright.

Drill 2–Toe In, Toe Out

Set course pylons the same as in *Drill 1.* Now we set about to unlock the hips. The team skates slowly around the outside of the course and when it reaches the blue line, have the boys lift one skate off the ice and glide straight ahead on the other. Say, for example, that they lift the right foot off the ice. They place the toe of the right foot against the toe of the left and turn the right heel outward as far as it will go. (24) They

24

should try to make a right angle with their feet, toe to toe, but few boys can get the heel out that far. They hold this position until they glide to the second blue line and skate away. On the other side of the rink, they lift the left foot and go through the same exercise.

After three or four minutes, change to toe out. This time they place the right heel against the left toe while gliding, and point the toe outward. (25) The boys find this drill much easier. Again, when they get around to the other side of the ice surface, they alternate feet.

When doing the toe in, boys have a tendency to twist the whole body in an effort to perform, and to veer off to one side. But their shoulders must remain at right angles to the boards, facing squarely ahead. Keep the speed slow.

25

26

Both positions, toe in and toe out, are important parts of more complicated drills to follow. Unless the player has the necessary flexibility in his lower body joints, he will have trouble with some vital skating movements.

Drill 3–Kick Three Times

This is another balance drill that helps unlock the hips. Follow the same course as in previous drills. Sticks are held in the top hand, pointing forward on the ice as in all skating drills.

Immediately on reaching the blue line, the player bends one knee slightly and kicks the other leg three times before putting it down on the ice, swinging it forward and backward on each kick. (26) (27) (28) He should reach as far forward and backward as he can. He skates away

after kicking and repeats the drill with the other foot on the opposite side of the ice.

The key here is bending the knee of the supporting leg. It acts as a

27

28

29

shock absorber and also maintains the balance. A lot of players will fall heavily in this drill, because they forget to bend the supporting knee and lose balance. Bending the knee

brings it over the ball of the foot, and once we get the shoulder lined up we are really making yards.

There should be no head bobbing or bending at the waist; all the action should be from the waist down. The boy's body should not bob up and down like a pump handle. By now you're getting a good idea of how much balance and flexibility the youngsters *don't* have.

Drill 4 – Skate with Both Feet on the Ice

This one helps to unlock the hips and starts to get the boy into the right power-developing position.

Stand with both feet at shoulder width, lift the right toe slightly and point it outward (toe out), and push with the heel. (29) As the boy starts to move, point the right toe inward again (30), describing a semicircle

30

31

on the ice with the right skate blade.
Return to starting position. (31)
Repeat the cycle, and pick up speed.

The idea is to propel the body,
without using body weight, by using
the power developed from the hips
down. The head and shoulders
should remain erect when developing power, The working foot should
not get behind the foot on the ice, or
it will have to be lifted clear of the ice
to get back into position. And the
idea is to make the boy propel
himself with both feet on the ice at
all times. When the boy is balanced
and performing properly, you should
note that his shoulder is over the
knee and over the ball of the foot.

The drill should then be repeated
using the left leg for driving power.

You will almost certainly have
boys lacking co-ordination and
balance who just can't catch on to it.
Take them to centre ice, make them

stand still, grasp one skate boot and
draw the semicircle on the ice with
it. Do the same with the other foot,
having the boy put pressure on the
heel each time. He will soon get the
idea and pick it up from there.

Drill 5–Lift leg, Sit, Get up again

This one is for balance, strength and
unlocking the hips. The pylons
remain in the same position as in
Drill 1, and the players skate the
same course, around the outside of
the markers.

Many boys (and even more adults)
think this one is impossible, but
nearly all of them will be able to
handle it by the third or fourth
practice. Basically it's the first drill,
the squat, with one modification. As
the player reaches the blue line at
slow speed, he lifts one leg out in
front of him, about one and one-half

32

33

34

to two feet off the ice, and squats on his heel. (32) (33) Get all the way down, not part way, because many players only dip their butt about six inches and then stand up when they feel thay are about to fall. Make them go all the way down until they do fall. When they've gone all the way down and balanced on one leg, have them stand up again and return the leg to the ice.

They should skate away and repeat the exercise, with the left leg raised, on the opposite side of the ice.

It takes balance to get down in this drill without falling, and balance, strength and co-ordination to get back up. Watch the same points here as in the first drill. Extend both arms forward, with the stick on the ice. The shoulder is over the knee, the knee over the ball of the foot. Nod the head forward. Once the boy

is able to get down without falling, he has the hang of it, needing only strength to get up again. Skates with poor support show up here. They just give out and the boy falls. The skate on the lifted leg must not touch the ice during any part of the drill.

Drill 6—Ride the Broom

This one is a lot of fun. It's a great drill for teaching balance and posture and the kids love doing it. Ignore the pylons and skate all over the ice.

The player skates fast, then grasping the top of his stick with both hands, he puts it between his legs and sits on the shaft. (34) (35) He coasts with the heel of the stick sliding on the ice, just like a witch riding her broom. He can turn himself by twisting the handle and

35

37

36

making the blade turn from side to side. (36)

Next he turns himself around from a front to a backward coast. (37) If the player has enough skill he can coast around the pylons at the end of the rink.

The skill is required in turning around backward. Ninety percent of the boys will fall the first time they try it, unless their skates are shoulder width apart and their weight is evenly distributed on the balls of the feet, not the heels or toes. It's another case of adopting the proper posture—shoulder over the knee, knee over the ball of the foot. When turning, the player must develop good control of his skates to prevent them from digging in and spilling him on the ice. This is another drill with which a boy with poorly fitting skates will have difficulty. It's always good for a laugh, especially if the instructor manages to fall when demonstrating, and the kids have so much fun they're not even aware of the teaching aspect.

Drill 7–Front Turn

Remove the pylons. This is an elementary turn that enables a player to turn around and reverse direction without veering off his original course. It's particularly useful for players who have taken a shot on goal. After shooting from a wing, many players make a turn into the corner from in front of the goal, thereby turning their backs on the play for a few moments. Using the front turn, a player is always facing the action and ready to take part in it.

38

We use it as an exercise for unlocking the hips, for toe in, toe out and the beginning of unlocking the knees. But it takes a great player to use it in a game.

The drill is broken down into three parts, and each one must be fully mastered by the player before it can be integrated into a completed turn.

In part one, the player takes three or four power-developing strides, and when at medium speed, starts to coast with both feet shoulder width apart. He then turns his hips and body to the left and begins to slide; both skates are now turned sideways, scraping the ice slightly as they slide. (38) If the body is properly balanced, in the right position, with the weight distributed evenly on each foot, the player should slide ten or 12 feet before stopping. He should leave a scrape mark along the ice about three or four inches

wide. This takes place *only* when the body is in the proper balance alignment; shoulders over the knee, knee over the ball of the foot.

Without the right alignment, everything goes wrong. Either the front foot or the back foot will dig into the ice and the player will stop too soon. Leaning too far forward or backward will have a similar effect, causing some pretty fancy contortions in an effort to stay upright. It should take only a few tries before the players get the right balance, turn their hips and slide, slide, slide.

Part two of the drill is sliding on the rear foot. Have all the boys stand still, and put arch to heel to form a 'T'. Then have them skate forward, lift the forward skate, and turn it toe out in the direction of the slide. Sit back to slide on the back skate with

39

41

40

the front skate still lifted off the ice. (39)

Now, as the slide begins to slow down, press down with your toe on the back skate. You start to go backward. (40) Once you're going backward, you put the right foot down onto the ice. (41) You're turning your hips and shoulders and should now be in a position to skate back in the direction you came. Now disengage your other foot from the ice, and bring it forward to take its stride in the new direction.

For this drill the players can use the full ice surface with no individual area. Once they have learned to complete the turn, they can immediately go into another one; the first three or four strides after coming out of one turn builds up speed for the next one. The instructors have to concentrate on individuals who are having trouble, and can stop the action to demonstrate for one or all if necessary.

Drill 8–Lateral Crossovers

This is a mobility drill that proves every boy is blessed with locked hips and knees, and two left feet. We're still trying to unlock those joints and improve balance. The player learns to walk sideways on his skates, lifting one foot over the other, a vital skill in backward skating.

But the drill is organized in such a way as to prove to the kids that it isn't as easy as it sounds. They have to be convinced that they can't do it after hearing the drill described.

First, explain to the team that you want them to take four steps sideways, in each direction. To the count of "one, two, three, stop" they (1) put the right foot over the left, (42) on the ice (2) bring the left foot back to a normal standing position (3) take a second step over the left with the right foot and (stop) bring the left foot back to its normal standing position. On the next counts, they reverse the process, starting with left skate over right, (43) right skate back to normal etc. They should return to the spot from which they started.

Note the correct side position for lateral crossovers. (44) The middle of the skate, not the toes, support the body weight.

Next, line the players up facing outward, evenly spaced along the boards from the goal line up towards centre. That, surprisingly, is the hardest job in teaching hockey.

In the past, I've spent 30% of the time allocated for a drill trying to get the boys evenly spread out. Oh how

42

they like to bunch up—as though the Good Humor Man was giving away ice cream at the blue line!

Assume again that you're working with 32 boys—that's 16 spaced at

43

44

them up on one side, you watch them skate across, and bunch up between goal line and blue line on the other side! So you scream "spread out!" "move down!" "use all the ice surface!"

You'll realize how important this is when you consider the dangers. The boys are backing up, and having so much trouble with their feet they haven't got time to see what's behind them. If they start out too close to each other, they run into one another when skating from side to side as shown in (45). I've had several boys who fell and were hit in the face by flying sticks. I've had a boy trip over another's hockey stick behind him, and severely bruise his tail bone; another cut his leg badly when he smashed into the kid beside him, sending both to the ice in a heap.

five foot intervals from goal line to red line.

Now pull out your hair—because, having spent two minutes setting

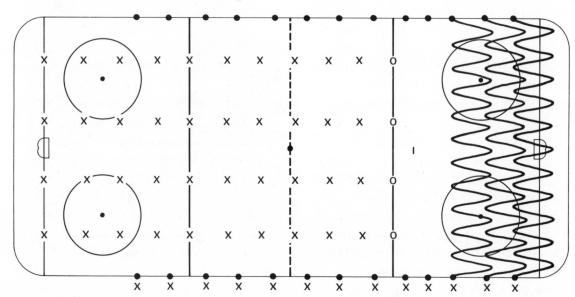

●   **Point of departure**
O   Pylons
X   Players
I   Instructor
45

Finally, a boy must start out after the player on his left is out 15 feet, otherwise the instructor can't give individual attention.

To solve the problem of spacing, I painted red dots at five foot intervals under the top rail on the boards. This didn't work satisfactorily until I numbered the spots on both sides.

Now let's continue. The players' sticks are held in one hand resting on the ice in front of them. Tell the team that their bodies must stay square with the boards during the drill, and start the boy on the goal line and the boy on the red line at centre ice first. When they are 15 feet out, start the boys to their right.

Start them off counting *one, two, three, stop; one, two, three, stop.* They will drift backward as they go, because they will walk on their toes, leaning forward to stare at those lumps below their ankles. By the time they have crossed the ice surface, having accumulated a few new bruises along the way, they are convinced it isn't so easy and the coach will have a standard by which to gauge progress in teaching the drill.

Don't even bother bringing them back across the ice; it's time to show them how it should be done.

Line them up with four players evenly spaced along the goal line, facing centre ice. See left side of rink (45). Put four more players about ten feet in front of them and so on, until you have about seven or eight rows of four players. (We practise two teams together because of a shortage of ice time, so in all these drills I'm working with about 32 boys. You can adjust your formation according to the number of players you have.)

The key to proper performance is taking the skating crouch with knees bent and back straight—shoulder over the knee, knee over the ball of the foot. And the steps *must* be taken flat-footed.

When doing the drill, the boys soon get out of line. When you first form the lines, put a pylon on the blue line in front of the first four boys—then they have a marker to go to when they regroup.

Count out loud and show them once:

One. Lift the right foot over the toe of the left and place it flat-footed outside the left skate. Now you're standing cross-legged.

Two. Take your left skate around behind the right and place it back in the normal standing position.

Three. Repeat step one.

Stop. Repeat step two.

Next do the drill in reverse, starting with the left skate over the right. Have the teams do the drill with the instructor and watch for these points: they have a tendency to turn the body in the direction they are going, so remind them to keep their body facing square to the front; they will lean forward to watch their feet when their torsos should be upright; they will forget how to count to four, so have them count out loud with you; their sticks will wander all over the place when they should be straight out in front. Keep their knees bent and their seats down, or they will be up on their toes when they should be flat-footed. Make them walk with you—slowly—if they run it's because they are not balanced.

As soon as they start to pick up the drill, speed up the tempo so they are doing it with a hop. On the way, the instructor can use pet phrases instead of the one, two, three, stop, tempo. ''Keep-your-head-up'', or, ''don't-turn-your-toes'', ''keep-your-back-straight'', ''get a little rhythm''.

This is the first drill where, by shifting the weight the player starts to develop power. It will come during the hop in backward skating. In about ten minutes, the instructor will have worked wonders. He can line the lads up along the boards and start at the top again, correcting each pair as they go. After a few minutes of this, they can go on to the next drill, but I suggest coming back to lateral crossovers repeatedly for more work, until all can do it. Next time back, you will have six boys who do it rather well, another six to nine who are awful. The other 20 will have an ''idea''—get your six best to go back to square one with your poor ones. The instructors should work with the 20 who are just coming along.

Drill 9—Back Skating
I can't emphasize enough how important this drill is—a boy cannot develop power from a stopped position unless he can turn his heel

out 90 degrees and sit and push. Nine boys out of ten—on every team from peewee to midget—can't develop full back-up speed from red line to blue line and then turn with an attacker. We simply do not teach our boys how to develop speed and thrust when backing up from a stop position. This drill is one of the keys. Work at it.

In this drill we want the player to skate backward from the hips down, not by transferring body weight from foot to foot or by wiggling his keester. The supporting leg should always be immediately under him in the shoulder over the knee, knee over the ball of the foot position.

Line the boys up, six across the goal line and five or six rows deep, facing the boards. Get them into the skating crouch with knees bent. Then they must turn the right heel out, (46) (47) and pressing on the

46

47

48

49

This allows the working foot to go through the full cycle of developing power. They repeat the exercise, using the right foot to propel themselves backward. Turn them around and make them use the left foot to propel themselves back.

The players must be checked for a tendency to transfer weight to the working foot. The instructor will constantly have to tap the supporting leg with his stick, making it stay directly under the boy's body. The player must learn to skate from his hips down, with no lateral movement of the torso or shoulders.

After the lads pick up the drill, have them practise it by skating around the full ice surface.

ball of the foot, cut a semicircle on the ice, returning the right skate to its place beside the left. (48) (49)

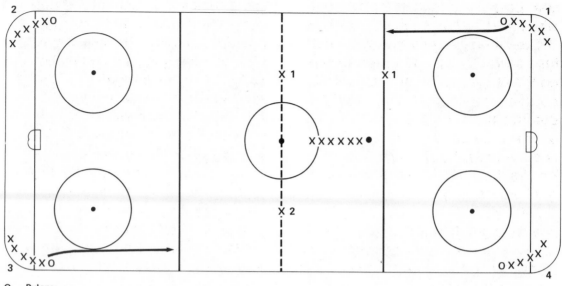

O   Pylons
X   Players

50

Drill 10—Back up, Turn, Pick Up, and Shoot

This is a drill I use as a selling point for teaching some of the skills outlined in earlier drills: backward skating and turns, toe in, backward push with the toe, and the four-part backward turn.

I've experimented on whether the skills should be given first, and then the one-on-one situation which utilizes them, or vice versa. What I do now is introduce this drill on the second day of teaching skills in hockey school, on the first day of teaching a hockey club.

It's a good drill also for the goal tenders' warm up, for a one-on-nobody or one-on-one situation, for down on one knee, down on two knees, for better stick control and many other areas.

With 20 skaters and two goal tenders, put five boys in each of the four corners, lined up behind pylons five feet in front of the goal line. Don't start the drill without 30 pucks.

Take the goal sticks away from your goal tenders, and when the boys skate out, first from *corners 1* and *3*, then from *corners 2* and *4*, have them aim high shots to make the goal tender use both hands in blocking and catching. Give him back his stick after three to four minutes and get the boys to either shoot or deke the goal tender.

Now line up your six defencemen on and behind the face-off spot in the centre ice area close to the blue line. (50) The defencemen take on only the boys approaching from *corners 1* and *4*. The boys from *corners 2* and *3* come down for the shot unmolested. Start out boys from *corners 1* and *3* simultaneously and start boys from *corners 2* and *4* only when the first two boys are finished.

The defenceman indicated with the *number 1* in the diagram stands on the red line until the attacker from *corner 1* reaches the blue line. The defenceman then backs up with the attacker, keeping him out of the scoring area. The boy from *corner 3* comes down the ice for a shot on goal unchecked.

Defenceman 2 moves to the red line as in the diagram, and tries to back up to stop the boy approaching from *corner 4*. The boy from *corner 2* comes down for a shot on goal unchecked. The defencemen return to their line by skating along the boards to the blue line, then out to their line-up.

Well, you have never seen anything so pathetic in your life. Unless the attacker is silly enough to skate right into the stumbling defenceman, the latter won't get close enough to hit the attacker with a handful of beans as he goes by. After I've tried everyone as defenceman, I'm lucky if one in 20 can put the attacker at a disadvantage.

Now let's get one thing straight. Any defenceman so challenged should be able to develop full power going backward in three to four strides; he should be able to turn and beat the attacker 99 tries in 100.

This drill proves once again that each kid has two left feet, bad posture and locked hips; so every second day we go back to the one-on-one situation to measure progress. However, we found that with 32 boys, there wasn't enough activity. The 12 defencemen (six on a team), had too long a wait before their turns came up to practise—in a

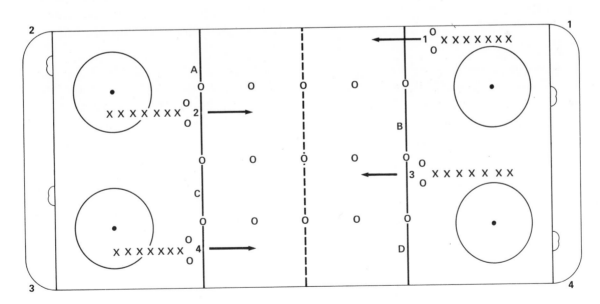

O Pylons
X Players

51

ten minute session they were lucky to get in ten game condition turns.

Here's what we cooked up. We took the pylons and split the rink in half length-wise, then into quarters. (51) We put a net and goal tender at the end of each, alternating ends as in the diagram. We placed the starting pylons four to five feet in front of the blue line in each area.

After we split the boys up into four groups we had each boy back up from his blue line until he crossed the red line. The first boy in each line skated backward from a stopped position until the red line was visible. He then turned toward the boards, picked up a puck at the blue line and went in to try and beat the goal tender. The boys must always turn toward the same boards—a player in *corner 1* would turn to his left on the return position.

The next player in line starts up when the first has picked up a puck—not a second earlier.

When finished, each player lines up in the line-up where they complete their drill. In this way, each two groups of four stay in their own half of the ice.

In doing five minutes of this drill, every boy had a chance to turn 25 times. Since every boy had a chance to beat a goal tender, as in a game situation, they put more effort into the drill.

And we even got a bonus. In going back to practise *toe in*, *toe out*, and other related back skating and turning drills, we found a renewed interest; when we got to the one-on-one situations, the kids' progress was encouraging instead of heartbreaking.

Drill 11–Backward Chop

I have a theory that our educational system has spoiled our kids in at least one respect—the only time they can use their brains is when they're sitting on their backsides. This is one of the first drills in which instructors will notice that as soon as the youngster becomes mobile, his brain stops. The proof will come in later, more complicated drills, but now we start unlocking their brains.

The *Backward Chop* teaches the players to develop power on the outside edge of the skate blade, really tests their balance, and unlocks hips and knees. The instructor should look for weaknesses, such as picking up the power foot before it has completed its cycle, not turning the foot out far enough, and lack of flexibility in the ankle, knee and hip joints.

The players start coasting backward with feet shoulder width apart. Lift the right foot at least nine to 12 inches off the ice (I have raised it a few feet in (52) to clarify the drill) and turn the toe out. (52) (53) Still coasting on the left skate, shift the body weight and lean to the left. (54) Just before losing balance, bring the upraised right foot across to the left and engage the ice *with the heel pointing outward, in the direction of the fall.* (55) The *toe out position must be maintained* as the right foot crosses in front of the left.

52

54

53

55

If the right skate engages the ice at the proper angle, the skater can transfer weight and push with the outside edge of the skate.

As the right skate develops power, the skater starts to lose balance to his right, and the left skate disengages the ice and repeats the cycle.

80

Again, the toe of the left skate must be turned out as it crosses in front of the right leg and engages the ice.

This is the only serious problem with this drill. Most boys bring the foot across as they do in the lateral crossover drill, with the toe pointed straight ahead. The blade will not be pointed at the angle at which the body is falling and a boy will not be able to pick up the rhythm necessary.

Once the boys realize they can't fall asleep during the exercise, and start concentrating, they catch on quickly. Then the coach should have them kick higher with the free skate and get the knee way up in the air; they will lengthen the time the power skate is on the ice.

Along about now many coaches will start to feel the little tingle in the spine. The earlier drills are starting to pay off. A team of youngsters performing the *Backward Chop* displays a considerable amount of grace and style. The legs kick high into the air with the rhythm of a can-can dancer, and this display is followed by a satisfying crunch as the skate bites deeply into the ice. Several times I've let good groups carry on the drill for a few extra minutes while I just sat back and watched. I'm sure they spotted the smug look on my face and started hamming it up a little for my benefit, putting a little extra kick in the leg and sway in the hips.

But it looks just great and can give a coach a little reward for his work. And I can honestly tell you, there are

a lot of pros who will find this just as hard to learn as the kids.

Drill 12–Backward Turn

The *Backward Turn*, I think, is the hardest skill for the boys to master, yet the easiest to teach. It's broken down into four individual movements and then put together into the complete turn.

Set out eight pylons as in *Drill 1*.

In the first movement, the players skate backward around the outside of the pylons and when they reach the starting pylon on the first blue line, they lift the right foot and turn it toe out, and coast straight back on the left skate. (56) If properly balanced on well-fitted skates, they will pick it up quickly. If not, they will wobble and go off course. Have the boys stay on one foot until they stop.

To create interest at this point, we

56

57

play 'cowboys and indians'. The skater tries not to leave a mark on the ice as he coasts backward. If balanced on the centre portion of the blade, he will not leave a mark on the ice. Then he is a 'smart indian'. Only a 'dumb cowboy' would leave a trail. If he leans head and shoulders forward and puts weight on the toe of the skate, or sits too far back on the heel of the skate, he will carve marks in the ice. Dumb cowboy!

In the second part of the drill, the skater moves his right foot from the toe out position to the arch to heel position.   The arch of the right skate is placed against the heel of the coasting skate to form a 'T'. Again, let them coast to a stop in this position.

Now you find that although the boy understands perfectly where the arch and heel are when he's stand-

ing still, his brain stops when he's on the move. You will have to stop the exercise at this point and get all the players to take the arch to heel position again, and personally inspect each one. Then start them off again and practise until they all get it; remember, there is no point in any boy progressing to the next part of a drill unless he has mastered the previous one.

Now for the third part. Get them going backward, and at the starting blue line, place arch to heel. Then the boys must turn their hips, shoulders and torso so they are facing centre ice as they coast from blue line to blue line. The instructor standing at centre should be able to see the front of the player's jersey as he goes by. (57)

When the player changes feet and repeats the drill on the opposite side of the ice, the instructor should be able to see the number on the back of his jersey.

When the skater turns his body to the right in step three, the heel of his right skate will almost automatically tuck itself further behind the heel of the left skate, and the right foot toe will point almost 180 degrees away from the left foot toe.

This takes great dexterity in the knees, pointing the toes in opposite directions, but the earlier unlocking drills should be paying off again. Remember, unless skates fit, are sharp, and the boy is in the shoulders over knees over ball of the foot position, there is no way he is going to do this.

58

59

The fourth part of the drill involves transferring weight to the right foot and completing the turn, but it includes the most important part of the drill—having the player come out of the turn faster than he went into it. The key is in part three. When the player turns his body to the right and points his toes in opposite directions, he will almost have to go into a semicrouch to facilitate the move. Any player who doesn't should be told to lower his seat just before going into part four.

Then at the moment of weight transfer to the right leg, the player digs in his left skate and pushes hard, fully extending the left leg. (58) (59) He should develop enough thrust to actually speed up on the turn. Just turning is not good enough; he must be able to accelerate.

The most common fault is stepping out with the right foot, which prevents the left leg from digging in; the player loses speed. He must push off right from the heel-to-heel position. The boys must also be made to execute more turns on one circuit of the ice. If left alone they will make one turn on each side of the ice. But they should be forced to make at least eight turns; three on each side and one turn on each end. They usually want to go too fast, but keep their speed down, make them perform slowly, and they will have time to make plenty of turns. Make them say to themselves—arch to heel—turn the hips and shoulders—sit down and push. When they sit down the turning skate engages the ice. So, after a four to five minute teaching period you have six boys who turn reasonably

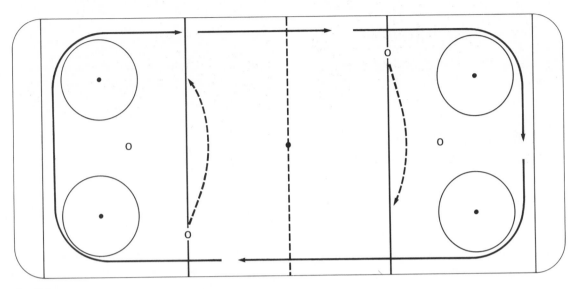

O   Pylons

60

well. Wait until you see them in game conditions—you will wonder where they lost it!

Drill 13–Back Skating on Turns
Set up four pylons. (60) One should be on each blue line close to the boards to force the players to use the full width of the end zone when turning. The wider and longer the turn, the easier it is.

Start the players skating backward the full length of the ice, doing *Drill 9*. They must do cross-overs when turning in the end zone. (61) They must be warned to watch where they are going by turning at the hips and looking to the inside, and to be responsible when they fall, for getting out of the way of approaching players.

Watch for two problems on the turns. Firstly, players lean too far forward, and get up on their toes.

They should keep their heads and shoulders back, and skate on the middle portion of the blade.

Next, they must learn how to bounce from the hips and shoulders on the turn. It's this rhythmic

61

bounce in each step that imparts speed. The ankles, knees, legs and hips supply the technique, and the shifting of body weight supplies the power on turns. If you keep the players off their toes, with head and shoulders back, they should improve quickly.

Have the players reverse direction. Remove the pylons from their positions on one end of the blue lines to the opposite end as shown by the arrows. Again, be sure the pylons are as close to the boards as possible. It's the only way to make the kids keep close to the boards.

Drill 14–Skating Analysis
This is a good time to find out how many of the players are developing those ball-bearing joints at the hips and below. This is also an excellent drill for doing a complete analysis of the players' skating technique.

The team skates slowly around the course. (62) As they approach the starting blue line on one side of the ice, they hold their sticks in both hands, (palms up), shoulder width apart, with arms fully extended shoulder high in front of them. (63) Note that the upper body is erect, the supporting leg straight under the skater.

As soon as they hit the starting blue line they skate full out, as fast as they can to the next blue line. They must try to hold the stick perfectly steady in the horizontal position when developing power. (64) You should be able to draw a vertical line from shoulder to knee to ball of the foot. In order to do this, the whole upper body must remain steady, particularly the arms and shoulders. The player must skate from the hips down only.

Now the coach watches for the following points:
● Is the supporting skate on the ice

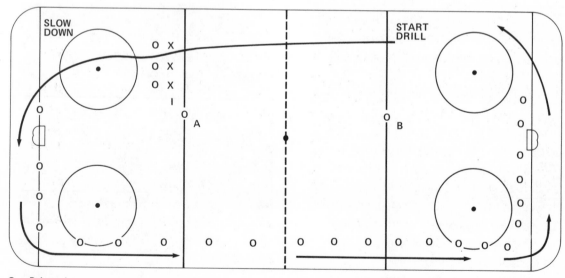

O   Pylons
X   Players
I   Instructor

63

directly under the player and if so, is he fully extending the working leg to develop power? (64) (65)

- Is the player turning his toe out, putting the maximum amount of

blade on the ice for good purchase?
- Is he running on his skates, not lowering his rear end far enough to get good mobility?
- Is the player's knee bent instead of straight when leaving the ice, or is he pushing with his toes only?

After the players go through the course and are corrected individually, pair them up and have them race against a partner. (62) It will make them lengthen their stride and become more conscious of shoulder weave by comparing their sticks with their partners'. Then they must really develop power from the hips down.

When the players complete their blue line to blue line stretch, they must be made to slow down and take their time between starting lines. Otherwise, they will tire after three or four times through the course.

Then the coach can put the team through the same drill carrying a puck, three at a time now, with both hands on the stick. (See diagram.) It's a good illustration to players and instructors, of how much easier it is to carry the puck in front of the body when the upper body is free of skating contortions. Set three pylons on the far blue line and have the players look at the pylons instead of the puck when skating the course.

64

65

Drill 15–Skating with One Leg

Skating with one foot on the ice is great for improving the ego.

Stand the player with both feet on the ice, then have him lift one foot off the ice and hold it in front of the body. Start skating backward with the other foot.

Then repeat, skating forward.

The player must have good balance, and good support in his skates. When the player can propel himself from this position, he is well on the way to developing power.

Drill 16–Jumping the Pylons

This is a great test for posture, balance, and the support given by the player's skates. The pylons are set out as in (66), lying on their sides, in pairs, and placed point to point.

The players start in the position shown on the diagram and skate at medium speed, one hand on the stick. The next boy starts when the fellow in front of him has completed the first jump. This is not a race.

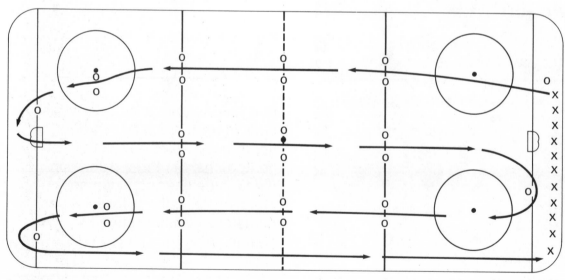

O   Pylons
X   Players

66

67

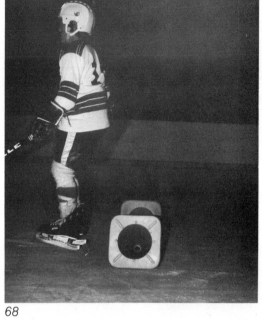

68

They approach the first pair of pylons coasting with both feet on the ice and jump over them, taking off and landing on both feet. (67) They will find it easier to jump high and maintain their balance if they keep the knees straight after takeoff and bend them again to absorb impact when landing, They should land on the centre portion of their blades, not on heel or toe, with head and shoulders back. (68) (69)

The players will find it difficult at first to take off and land on both feet; they will usually try to sneak in a step, taking off on one foot and landing on the other.

After clearing one set of pylons they take another stride, coast up to the next set, jump, and continue through the course.

After one or two circuits of the course, move the pylons together, point to base, increasing the height of the jump. The players repeat the same course.

Next, move the pylons point to

69

point again and put the players through, taking off and landing on one foot. The aim is to have the boys jump the entire row of three or four pylons on one foot. A reward comes in handy here. You should also move the pylons one length to one side, to use uncut ice. This helps considerably during the one-footed jumps.

Alternate the feet on each leg of the course, giving equal time to left and right. After a couple of tries, reward all the players who make the course successfully with a soft drink. Those with good support and balance will pick up the drill quickly, and they will all do it in time.

Practising the Drills
If you use my suggested method of devoting the first half hour of practice time to basic drills and the second half to doing your own thing, you will get a lot more accomplished in the 30 minutes than you may expect.

I suggest an average of five minutes for each drill, but that can be flexible according to the ability, age and condition of the players. But after experiencing the usual organizational problems, you might get through only the first three skating drills—*Squat, Toe in, Toe out,* and *Kick Three Times*—before running out of time.

Then, as the players learn the drills, you can spend less time with each one; five minutes the first week, four minutes the next and so on. But even when the team

becomes quite proficient at any drill, do not drop it for any length of time. You must not start believing that the value of elementary drills diminishes as the player advances through the more complicated exercises.

There are teams that started my skating drills five years ago and still spend at least one and one-half minutes at each of them during practices.

My philosophy draws a comparison between young hockey players and most of the world's best professional musicians. Ask any concert pianist how much time he or she spends running through the scale *do, re, me, fa, so, la, te, do.* It was probably the first musical exercise learned, but it still gets constant practice time.

I have a feeling that quite a number of youngsters in my minor hockey system can end up in professional ranks if they want to. If I'm still around when they get there, I'll still be on their backs if they neglect the basic skills.

As his practice program develops, the coach will be able to spend less and less time on the first drills and use the extra time for the introduction of new drills. Eventually he will be able to get 12 to 15 or more drills in each practice period and cover all the drills, including puck handling and passing, in two or three practice periods.

During games the coach will spot many weaknesses (e.g, defencemen whose sloppy backward turns allow opposing forwards to get past them) that will require concentration on certain basic drills in the next practice. Almost without exception, mistakes made during a hockey game can be traced back to a deficiency in a basic skill. Practise that skill, and you will correct the mistake.

4
Puck Control

One of the most admired, and the rarest abilities in a hockey player is good puck control. Intricate passing, booming shots, and stiff checking are great crowd pleasers, but nothing brings the crowds to its feet faster than the sight of someone, like Max Bentley, dipsy-doodling through an entire opposing team as if the puck was an extension of his stick.

To me the ability to stickhandle is the most exciting skill in the game. One would suppose that because this ability is so rare it is either difficult to learn, or has been made obsolete by the 'skate and push' technique that prevails today. Which one is true? Neither one, my friend.

I found puck handling difficult when I was in the N.H.L. because no one had ever showed me how, and I couldn't figure it out myself. As for being obsolete, well, the name of the game in professional hockey now is making money. If someone can convince me that skating and pushing the puck is a better crowd pleaser than brilliant stickhandling, or that it's a better way of keeping the puck away from the opposing team, then I'll buy them a gold plated key to the hockey analysts' washroom at the Montreal Forum.

Stickhandling has been referred to as the forgotten art of the game since the day after hockey was invented. It wasn't forgotten, it was simply never learned by most players. How many old timers today can recall the names of the great stickhandlers of the past, and get

past the fingers of one hand?

Good puck handlers are made, not born. Most hockey players and coaches will not believe that, but if I can convince them to teach kids just the basic skills of puck handling, a lot of those youngsters will have enough knowledge to go all the way.

Give any kid a good basic knowledge of any hockey skill and nine times out of ten he'll be smart enough to figure the rest out for himself as he grows up in the game.

The Hockey Stick

If a well-fitted skate boot is fundamental to good skating, the hockey stick is equally important to good puck handling. If the stick doesn't fit the kid, everyone is wasting his time. The stick has to be the right length and lie.

Grip
The top hand must be right at the end of the stick, not several inches down the handle. The wrist should be turned over so far that the 'V' formed between the thumb and forefinger points at the right shoulder, if a player is right handed.

The lower hand should be ten to 13 inches down the handle, with the palm over the top of the stick, not against the side. Again, the 'V' between the thumb and forefinger should point at the right-hand shoulder if the player is a right-handed shot. (70)

70

71

The key here is keeping the elbow of the lower arm on the stick straight. When standing in the normal stickhandling position, with blade on the ice, the straight elbow should force the player into the proper hockey-playing position. The proper hand grip and straight elbow are also necessary to allow the player to roll his wrists—the deep,

dark, but simple secret of controlling the puck. (71)

Rolling the wrists
If you watch youngsters stickhandling, you will notice that while they flip the puck back and forth nicely in front of them, they will invariably lose it, after a few moments, off the toe or heel of the stick. Look again and you'll see that in all cases the blade of the stick is pointing straight ahead when the puck is lost. This happens when the player's wrists are frozen or locked on the stick.

Watch the player who seldom loses the puck when stickhandling, and you'll see he is cradling or cupping the puck with his stick. That player is rolling his wrists.

Puck control is the ability to roll the wrists. Try it. Pick up a stick and stand in the stickhandling position. If you're on the living room floor, use a ball or rolled up piece of paper for a puck. Hold your wrists steady and stickhandle the puck back and forth in front of you.

Next, after sliding the puck (or ball) to the left, roll the wrists so the toe of the stick turns inward and the heel goes outward before intercepting it. Then, instead of passing the puck back to the right, roll the wrists in the opposite direction and flip the puck on the ice. The toe of your stick will then point to the left and the heel toward the right, and it will be in position to intercept the puck on the right side of your body.

Speed up the action and you'll see what I mean about cupping or

94

72

73

cradling the puck as you stickhandle.

There is no way you can lose the puck while stickhandling if you roll the wrists and cradle it properly. The puck will always be held in the centre portion of the blade or the fulcrum of the rolling action, and in position for shooting or passing.

Puck Handling Drills

Drill 1–Skating Backward and Rolling Wrists

Line the players up with feet shoulder width apart in the stickhandling position with a puck in front of them. Have them put the heels of their sticks about one or two inches above the puck, rolling their wrists so that the tip of the blade touches the ice on each side of the puck. (72) (73) This is an exaggerated movement but keep them at it for several minutes until they all get the idea of rolling the wrists.

Place the pylons as on page 61 and have the boys skate around the course backward, carrying the puck with two hands on the stick. The puck should be at the middle of the body, not at the side.

Blow the whistle. Have them take the top hand off the stick, and, carrying the puck backward, keep it in front of the body, not beside. (74) (75) If the stick is too long, they can't skate backward with only the bottom hand on the stick and the blade flat on the ice.

Blow the whistle again, and repeat the exercise with just the top hand on the stick.

If the players roll their wrists, the puck must come along with them; they'll have no further doubts that it can be done.

On second thought, instead of going from goal line to goal line, have them go from goal line to blue line and back again. The strain on

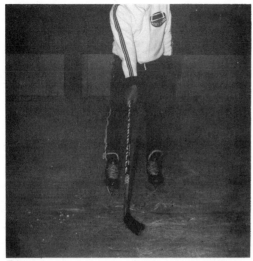

74

75

the wrists at the longer distance is too great.

Drill 2—Two-footed Stop

Now we advance into somewhat more complicated drills involving skating, puck carrying and shooting. It's important that the boy stickhandle the puck through all future drills by rolling his wrists. There may be

times when it will be necessary for him to skate and push the puck, but if he is catching on to skating from the hips down, he will be developing almost as much speed as when he swung his shoulders and arms wildly—and had to give away the puck while doing it.

But now the kids will have an awful lot to remember while skating with the puck, and if they stop thinking—and they sure as heck will—the coach must be prepared to have the drills screwed up regularly. We still have a long way to go in unlocking their brains when moving.

This drill teaches the boy to stop, using both feet, on the left and right sides of the body. If not properly balanced, he will use just one foot, front or back, and will probably fall. The skill is to glide on both skates as he approaches the stopping point, then turn the hips and body at right angles to the direction in which he is moving, lower the rear end and sit. The feet should be shoulder width apart when he starts and finishes the stop. The squatting action drives the blades into the ice, while the weight is on the centre section of the blades.

After the players learn the technique, it will not be necessary to glide before stopping. They will be able to put on the brakes fast from a full stride and develop a pumping down action to dig the skates in. When doing this drill, and all puck handling drills, make sure the boys keep *two* hands on the stick—*always, always, always.*

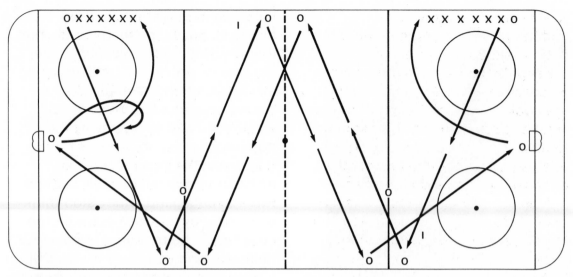

O Pylons
X Players
→ Direction of course
I Instructor

76

See (76) for the pylon layout and course skated. The players skate from the pylon close to the goal line to the pylon opposite at the end of the blue line to the pylon opposite at the end of the red line to the pylon opposite at the end of the blue line, and then go in for a shot on goal. It's very important that the players stop at the pylon which is five feet short of the end of each line using the two-footed stop. There's a danger of collision once the players are skating around the course in both directions; ten feet between players is never too much.

After a player comes to a full stop at the end of each line, he takes off for the end of the next line across the rink. The second player starts when the first boy passes the pylon on the blue line, one-quarter of the way to the second pylon. This can be adjusted to speed up or slow down the goalkeeping action. They have to be so well spaced that the shots on the goalkeeper do not come too fast. The coach must also ensure that the players alternate their stops, on the left and right sides of the body.

When the players complete the first half of the course they line up along the boards again and skate a course parallel to the first one on the return trip.

After the boys complete the course several times, so that they are thoroughly familiar with it, add this dimension to the drill.

The first player finishing takes a shot on goal. He then waits in the attacking area, way out in front of the net, to take a pass from the next man just starting up from the last pylon and it becomes a two-on-nobody situation. The first player then leaves to take his place in the line, as number two waits for number three, for another two-on-nobody situation, and so on.

Keep the players skating as fast as possible while they stickhandle the puck in front of them (not to one side) or push it ahead and catch up. An instructor should be placed at each stopping point to correct them because the whole drill (and any drill) is a waste of time unless everything is done right. Check to be sure the player has both hands on the stick.

Coaches may find that the players catch on to the course faster if there is no goal tender in the net for the first couple of circuits. Although the course is simple, most youngsters find it takes all their concentration to complete the course, without the added pressure of worrying about beating the goalie. If I have a really green class, I put the goalie in after they have learned the circuit. The

kids also start learning to keep their heads up after their first collisions at the stopping points.

Drill 3—Skating the Circles

This is a good maneuverability, discipline, thinking and balance drill that teaches the player to carry the puck and develop power while doing crossovers. The trick is to get two players on each circle, so that when they are working from both directions, most of the 30 boys can be moving at once.

Set out the pylons and line up the boys. (77) You may find it necessary to mark the course between *circles 2, 3* and *4* with pylons and to set pylons where they are to line up for the return circuit.

If you practise two teams as we do, line the boys up in alternate coloured jerseys. (77) Warn them that anyone skating *circles 1, 2,* or *3* who runs into a defenceman

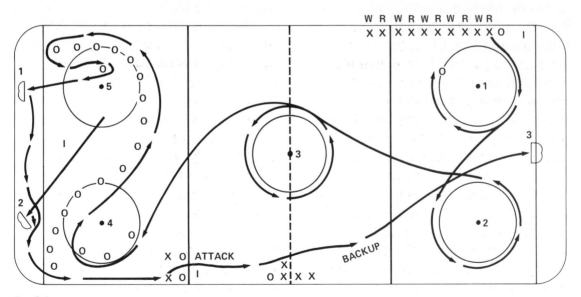

O Pylons
X Players
I   Instructor

77

backing up in a two-on-one situation, had better beat you to the exit, because if he doesn't, he just won't get through that gate alive.

We put this drill together while waiting for the fog to clear in the arena when we were doing the CBC instructional films in St. John's, Newfoundland. The parents and hockey followers who saw it for the first time had a fit. Someone was going to get killed for sure, they thought.

Do you know that we have done the drill six times a day for 90 days with boys from nine to 16 years of age and they accepted the challenge? I can't remember one defenceman being clipped or tripped by anyone, or one kid shooting on *net 1* being hit by someone shooting on *net 2* as he joined the boys for the return trip up the ice.

A professional player almost had a fit when he first saw the exercise, but when he, like others, realized that the kids favourably responded when challenged, he grew to like the drill.

My biggest challenge has been to create something of interest for the goalers while teaching skills to the players. This drill keeps three goal tenders as busy as one-armed paper hangers.

The key is to set the pylons and start the players properly. The second boy starts out when the first reaches the pylon on *circle 1.* If you encounter a traffic jam in the goal area, adjust the pylon on *circle 1.* White jerseys, after rounding the *circles 1, 2, 3, 4,* round the pylon

deep in the corner and cut sharply to go around the pylon near the face-off circle. (*circle 5*). They then shoot on white goal tender (*Number 1*). Boys in red jerseys fire at the red (*Number 2*) goal tender.

The forwards wearing white jerseys, careful to stay out of the red jerseys' line of fire, now head for the two pylons at the blue line area. The defencemen head for the single pylon at centre ice and line up along the fence. The two forwards, with one defenceman skating backward before them, now play a two-on-one situation against the third goal tender.

If no defenceman is ready, the two forwards play a two-on-nobody situation. Talk about a traffic jam at the blue line!

Look at the overall picture. You have two fellows on *circle 1,* two on *circle 2*, two on *circle 3*, and one going from *circle 2 to 3.* There are seven fellows, each with a puck, skating all out upstream, and two boys on one defenceman skating down. Lots of collisions, but to date, that fellow skating backward has never been hit.

And I haven't had to scream ''keep-your-head-up!'' more than once or twice. Somehow the kids seem to sense that if they look for nickels, someone is going to lower the boom. The drill just dares someone to fall asleep. If he does, he pays the price. Have the red and white goal tenders change nets during the drill and see how many players pick it up. Those looking for nickels won't!

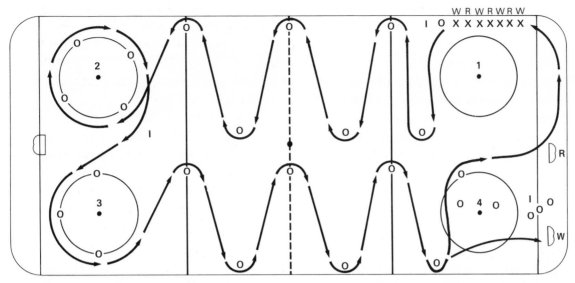

O   Pylons
X   Players
I   Instructors

78

Don't let their success go to their heads; just turn them around and put them through the course skating backward with the puck until they meet the last pylon in the corner, then turn, shoot, and continue the drill in the usual way. And rack up a few more gray hairs.

Drill 4—The Pylon Game

This is probably the best drill for developing puck control, balance, skating power, game sense and goal tending.

The course has to be set up as in (78) for the drill to work properly. And it's the best drill you can use to reason with a player about the length of his hockey stick.

After the first several times through the course, the coach will be convinced the players didn't get a thing from all the previous skating drills. A coach can look for and find

poorly-fitted skates, blades too dull, sticks too long, inability to cross legs over, inability to roll the wrists, inability to turn on two feet, inability to sit to develop power, inability to skate with two feet on the ice, developing power by shifting body weight or swaying, instead of using muscles from the hips down, inability to skate backward and inability to carry the puck.

On the brighter side, if the player can stump you on most or all of

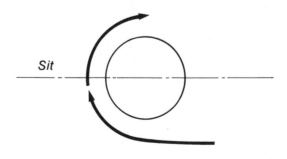

79

these points, he's quite a puck handler and skater.

Forehand Approach

There is quite a technique to going around a pylon properly. It takes considerable skating and puck handling skill. The player wants to take the shortest route around a pylon, so that when he approaches one on his forehand, (a right-handed player rounding a pylon on his right), he takes the puck on the backhand side of his stick. The player glides with skates shoulder width apart for the last couple of feet. When his body comes even with the pylon, (79), he sits lower, and, with his outside skate, develops power by turning toe out and pressing with the heel. This should bring him out of the turn faster than he went into it. He should have added enough speed to coast 15 feet past the pylon, turn around, coast back, and go around it again. He can keep this up all day without lifting his outside skate off the ice.

Now a new puck handling trick must be taught. When a player standing in the normal puck handling position bends his knees, the toe of the stick lifts off the ice. When he is in the power-developing position while skating, his knees are bent even further and the toe of the stick can lift two or three inches off the ice. (80) But when a player is going around pylons, he is leaning to the inside, and sitting and push-ing to develop power, which means there is no way a kid will be able to

80

81

hold on to the puck. No way, that is, if he keeps his elbows in their normal positon at his sides.

The deeper a player crouches, *the higher he must raise his elbows* in order to keep the blade of his stick on the ice, and keep control of the puck. (81) This skill has to be learned by any player who follows my techniques, because nearly all skating and puck handling is performed in a semicrouch.

Backhand Approach

When a player approaches a pylon on his backhand side (a right-handed player rounding a pylon on his left) he will not be able to carry his stick and the puck in the normal position, for the puck will roll off the end of his stick as he makes the sharp turn. Even if he rolls his wrists to the maximum, the odds are he will still lose the puck. The puck has to go around first, ahead of the player, if he is to keep it under control.

A right-handed player must move his top hand, the left, out away from his side and bring it across the front of his body to the outside of his bottom hand. A player can't perform this maneuver if his stick is too long or if he has not developed good balance. Once again, he has to keep his elbows high to keep the stick blade on the ice.

When starting the players through the course, it helps to keep them better spaced by moving the first set of pylons a little deeper than the rest. The first player moves out from the starting position along the boards, stickhandling the puck in front of him. As he *goes around* the first pylon, the next player starts. The pylons marking the turning positions along the boards should be moved occasionally, as the ice gets cut up and makes puck handling more difficult. The first time through, the players should skate with both skates on the ice,

which helps remind them to keep both skates on the ice when rounding the pylons.

The coach will really have to work on the kids who have not picked up the technique of skating with both skates on the ice. It can be really frustrating, but he has to give them a stick and puck and a prescribed course to follow on their own, keeping them at it until they improve. At this point, the coach should realize the importance of making sure every player can do every drill before he moves on to the next one. It doesn't really slow the group down much, especially if the coach uses the better kids to help the slower ones. But the whole exercise really breaks down when players who have not mastered the basic drills get involved in the more complicated variety.

You will run into difficulty at *circle 2* and *3*. An instructor between these two circles should help direct traffic.

After the players have learned the course, start making it more interesting. If you have 30 boys or more at a practice, use two goal tenders. Line up the players in alternating red, white, red, white jerseys. Have the white jerseys attack on the white, the red attack on the red goal tender. Then return to position for another time through. (78) A boy who shoots on *goal 1* must be careful when he goes back to line up, that he stays out of the line of fire at *goal 2*.

Next they must skate the course with normal strides, and with this added speed, it all breaks down again. I don't want to discourage new coaches, I'm just telling it the way it is when working with youngsters. Just by adding speed, the players will start to round pylons on only one foot, they will not sit down for power, they will forget to roll the wrist and will lose the puck . . . well, just keep them at it and they will improve.

Finally, move the pylons further away from the boards and make them go through the course skating backward, then eventually, backward carrying the puck. Yup, they'll do it.

Drill 5–Raising the Elbows

When I first watched the Russians practice for the 1972 Canada-Russia Hockey Series, I wondered why their finest players, when carrying the puck in warmups or going in one on goal, went down on one knee, then on two knees when they hit the red line and blue line. Sometimes they even passed from that position, then got up and finished the play.

First I thought it was for balance, then for puck control, but for six months it bothered me. There had to be a more direct, logical reason.

Rightly or wrongly, many of us feel the Russians passed better than the Canadians and, (which is just as important), received better. We Canadians miss so many passes because we have not mastered the skill of keeping the full blade of the stick on the ice when reaching for the puck.

I've been able to talk to kids about raising the elbows, and demonstrate how it keeps the stick blade on the ice, but I've never been able to devise a skill-teaching situation that would force the boys into the habit. So that Russian drill kept bugging me until one day it finally soaked in. Thanks to the Soviets I now have the drill.

I first started teaching this drill using the entire ice surface for 32 to 36 boys and two goal tenders. I placed eight boys in each corner and one goal tender at each end.

The players started from their opposite corners simultaneously first from *corners 1* and *3*, then, when they have finished their play on net, those from *corners 2* and *4*. When they hit the red line, they went down on one knee and stickhandled with the puck in front of the body, keeping the full blade of the stick on the ice. (82) After a ten or 15 foot glide, they got up and went in for a shot on goal. They then lined up in

82

the opposite corner for another turn.

I stood on the blue line. The players approaching me in front went down on their right knees, those approaching from behind went down on their left. It helps body control and direction if the boy drags the toe of the trailing skate on the ice. If he turns his foot, there are problems.

It is important to make the boys aware of what their wrists, hands and elbows have to do to allow full blade-puck control.

Before Russia, I would have been happy with this drill—two boys rushing from each right side, followed by two rushing from each left. But it bugged me no end that we had 30 boys standing and falling asleep, while just two kids and two goal tenders used the full ice surface. A kid had to wait until

seven fellows had a rush before his turn came up.

Why not divide the rink down the centre using four nets, with only four guys to a corner instead of eight? To keep from getting their heads taken off by a wayward shot on goal, all the kids had to do was move up and away from the goal mouth action. If they did not—they paid the penalty.

So we took 18 pylons, split the rink down the centre, dressed three goal tenders and dug out one practice board. (83) Away we went, four in each corner, one instructor on each surface. Worked perfectly. We just banned slap shots.

After three or four minutes of down on one knee, it was down on two knees, stickhandle, get up and shoot. No standing—no waiting—lots of action. After the right corners had

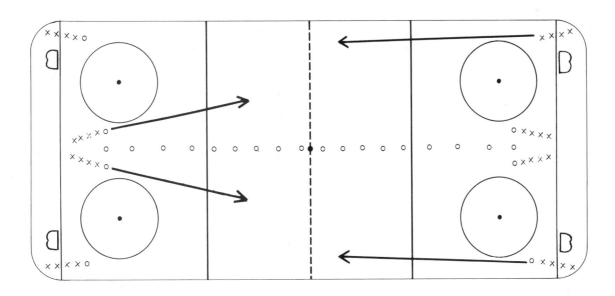

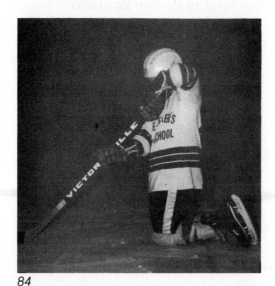

84

gone through it, the left corners did the same.

Later, we moved the left corners down to join the right, pairing them up six or eight feet apart. The puck carrier at the red line went down on one knee or two, (84), then passed the puck to his team mate.

The passing drill seemed to work better for getting the elbow and

wrist up, forcing the top hand well away from the hips. The slow ones soon realized to either get the top hand up, or no pass. It also forced a player into using a stick that was closer to the proper length.

If a coach is working with 20 players, the entire ice surface may be used. (85)

Players from *corners 1* and *3* start together. When they are attacking their goals, players from *corners 2* and *4* start out. Players from *corner 1* go to *corner 3*, those from *corner 3* line up in *corner 1* when finished. Players from *corners 2* and *4* do the same, lining up in each other's end when finished.

If you ever find out how to stop boys from starting out from all corners at the same time, please write.

Drill 6–Stickhandling, Puck Control and Goal Tending
If you've done your homework and taught the boys to develop power

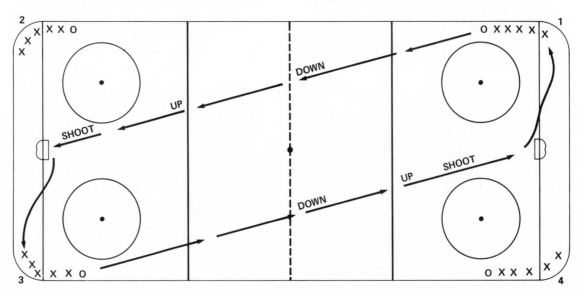

85

from the hips down, there's really no need for them to ever take the bottom hand off the stick. Yet I'm forever screaming at them to keep their bottom hands on their sticks when carrying the puck.

Why? Because the hands are not in the stickhandling position and the elbow on the lower arm is bent instead of straight. With hands too far apart and elbow bent, the boy is forced to bend at the waist, and any extended time in that position brings on a sore back. To relieve this, a kid takes the lower hand off the stick, straightens the back—and watches the puck sail underneath the toe or off the heel of the blade.

This drill forces the kids to keep both hands on the stick, eyes ahead. And there's a bonus. You can slip in a great piece of goal tending action to keep those guys from standing around doing nothing, or just going through the motions of carrying a puck.

Split your team in half; put one group between blue line and red line on each side of centre. (86) Give each boy a puck and have them skate against each other in circles. (See direction of arrows in (86).) Keep them between the blue lines: you want a close-quarter, jammed situation.

Those boys who take the stick to the ice by bending the back instead of the knees, those with a low lie stick, hands too far apart and elbow bent, will have the lower hand off the stick in less than a minute while the others, with proper grip and posture, will laugh their way through it for up to five minutes. Here's your chance to teach the proper way to hold the hands and elbow when stickhandling.

The goal tenders stand where marked. (86) When the skater comes in and tries to stickhandle the puck through or by him, he slides his stick out and tries to stick

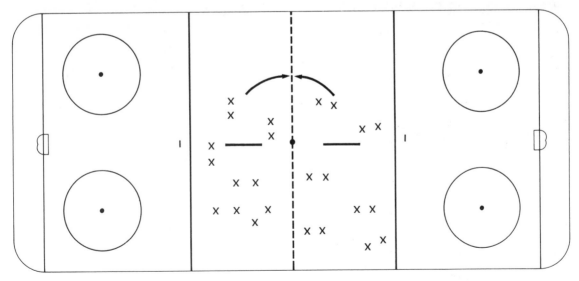

X   Players
——   Goal tenders
I   Instructor

86

check the attacker. It's an excellent stick control drill for the goal tender and a great teaching situation.

And here's another bonus: with so much traffic between the two blue lines, the boy learns to keep his head up, or suffer the penalty.

An observant coach will have to notice during the puck handling drills, that any youngster who has not learned the basics of skating will be a washout. The coach will have to constantly harp on the key areas of skating: good ankle support, sharp blades, good balance, and developing power through long strides, hip action and shifting weight.

Similarly, he must constantly stress key areas of puck handling: right length of stick, proper grip, ability to roll wrists, ability to keep the stick blade on the ice in the manner described in *Drill 5*.

5
Passing and
Pass Receiving

The Art of Passing

I Learned the Hard Way

It is of utmost importance that every boy understand at least the mechanics of making a pass thoroughly. Not all of them will acquire the skill, mind you, but those who do will take their place among the top players on any team. Every boy deserves the chance to learn how to pass, but it presents one of the most perplexing problems in my hockey experience.

I played in the N.H.L. for eight years, was a member of four Stanley Cup teams and even won the *Rookie Award*, yet I drove linemates Ted Kennedy, Vic Lynn and later, Cal Gardner and Harry Watson, crazy. I couldn't pass the puck out the Zamboni gate from 20 feet away.

I read every instructional book I could lay my hands on and talked to most of the best coaches of the day, and the best advice I could get was ''keep your eye on the target and follow through at the target.'' No one ever mentioned 'feel' so I was a head dropper. My passing was 'by guess and by God'.

I never had much luck at finding someone to teach me to pass, so at 35 years of age, I figured it was time to work the whole thing out for myself. Before I take you through parts of that self-learning process, I must warn coaches that they are about to enter the most difficult and frustrating aspect of the game.

To teach passing is work that will test any man's perseverance. At times he will be sorely tempted to go on to teaching game philosophy, but he would be doing the boy and the game a disservice if he abandoned passing for, say, shooting.

My big problem in passing is motivation. If any coach ever finds an answer to that one I'd appreciate hearing about it. I've found that I can get almost 58 minutes of concentrated physical and mental effort from all players out of one hour and 15 minutes of skating and puck handling instruction. So, although it's hard work for two instructors to keep 30 boys interested in these drills for an hour, it can be done.

A boy may stay interested because he feels himself getting better, stronger on his skates, mastering one or two new drills each day while in my hockey school. Both the student and teacher can measure such progress on an almost day-to-day basis.

But I haven't been able to sustain that degree of interest and dedication in passing.

It's been suggested to me that kids of this age, though not conscious of it, are too selfish to pass the puck. In their young minds, no one has really become a star in the big time until he has led the scoring parade; success is scoring goals. Unconsciously, he doesn't want to give that puck to someone else. All the glory is heaped on the guy who scores goals, so how is a kid going to be noticed among all the others if he gets to be an expert at giving the puck to someone else? The boy, so the suggestion goes, is not mature enough to realize that his wing-mate, by also becoming a good passer, will return the puck as often as he receives it.

I'm not qualified in child psychology to comment on this suggestion, but I do have a theory of my own. The more time I spend with passing drills, the more convinced I become that the educational system is the root of the problem.

Almost from day one in school, as I mentioned before, the only time a boy is asked to think, to really get the brain moving, is when he is sitting on his keester. The second the student gets on his feet and starts to move, the brain's power of concentration decreases.

The biggest and toughest job for the teacher of hockey is to get the brain working and keep it working, not to acquire skills (though that helps) but to get fellows with average intelligence to learn the general routine of a certain skill drill.

You can get boys to perform a passing skill perfectly while standing still. But get them mobile, and if the skill has four individual phases, they will forget three of them. And remember, this happens with greater frequency as you increase the tempo of the exercises and get closer to game conditions. Don't ask me how I've solved the problem; I haven't.

But I do think that 70% of all teaching to boys up to 12 years of age should be aimed at skating and

puck handling. And here I am including the average Canadian minor hockey league system, which is based on hockey for everyone, both recreational and competitive, with the most talented getting what they deserve—ice three times a week, good instruction and competition.

During the growing years, ages 13 and 14, is the time to perfect skating and puck control and to teach passing. And at ages 15 and 16, it's soon enough to concentrate on game philosophy and to continue work on passing.

But, as I said, all players must be given a chance to learn the basics; everyone's passing can be improved to some degree. Those who are willing to work at it, and have good balance plus a little hockey ability, can become deadly accurate in both forehand and backhand.

The Principle of Passing
The self-learning process began after my arrival in Newfoundland. And my big breakthrough came, not on the ice, but when involved in Newfoundland's annual fall ritual, the moose hunt. Every season my boys and I zero in with our .270 moose rifles. One day I was sitting with an old American air force buddy who had much experience in gun handling, talking about muzzle velocities, trajectories,etc. I was half watching my son, away off to the right, line up his rifle with the target when I suddenly started to relate his actions to hockey. That wasn't an

unusual thought switch for me; there's not a day in the year when I don't spend some time thinking about hockey. My friends think I'm a bit of a nut about it.

The flight path of a bullet—and passing . . . I realized that at the moment of bullet release, when my son squeezed the trigger, the face of the barrel had to be square with the target. If it was, the bullet had to be on target. It could be high or low, but not out of line.

If a stick blade was square with the target at the exact instant of puck release, the puck had to be on target. There was no way it could be otherwise. I had just discovered what thousands of other people already knew, but I still felt like Alexander Graham Bell.

How I managed to stay for the rest of the hunting trip I don't know, but I couldn't wait to get on the ice with a group of boys and try it out. I spoiled the first hour of ice time in the season for the kids on the Holloway School peewee hockey team when I made them do nothing but pass the puck to a buddy from a standing and moving position.

It's funny what you can see when you look from a totally new perspective. The first serious problem I encountered was that the sticks were all too long. This turned out to be a tremendous handicap in passing, and even more so in receiving. With the long stick, the player's top hand was locked at the side of his body when he put the full length of the blade on the ice.

When I got the pass receiver to present a target with his stick blade, the passed puck was constantly going into the receiver's skates or several feet in front of his stick. When I watched the passer closely I found that the only hand he moved was the bottom hand on the stick. I started to relate the gun barrel to the hockey stick at the moment of release, and discovered that the only time the blade was square with the target was at the beginning of stick movement. Nearly all the players started the pass from the centre line of their bodies, or in front of them. Then the player would sweep the puck toward the target, and before the puck disengaged from the blade, the blade was no longer square with the target.

The player 'aimed' his pass the same way I and I suppose many others did: by rolling the puck off the end or near the end of the blade, directing its path at the last second.

O.K. We found out what was wrong with that method of passing, but how to remedy it? The obvious answer was to move both hands, top and bottom, at the same time instead of just the lower hand. That would keep the blade of the stick square with the target throughout the swing. But that skill was way beyond the ability of our average beginners.

So we tried having the passer move the puck well behind the centre line of his body and start the pass from there. Eureka! When he started the pass from in front of his rear foot, the blade travelled eight to ten inches before the puck disengaged—just when it was perfectly square with the target. The puck zeroed in on the target as if it had eyes.

But there was still something wrong. I kept thinking "nothing exciting is happening. As many pass receivers as ever are turning and chasing loose pucks even though they're right on target." So I started watching the pass receiver.

The Holloway team was lined up facing each other in pairs along the red line and blue line. Passer and receiver each straddled his respective line with his feet on the outside edges of the line. This position, I found, was the best way to teach the passer to take the puck behind the centre line of his body before passing. If he moved the puck back to the outside of the blue line or red line, the release point would be at the centre of the line when the blade was square with the target.

So the pass took off straight for the receiver's blade. But the receiver's stick, when the pass arrived, would 'give' with the puck and as the blade went backward it opened up, letting the puck slide off the end or under the toe. Then the kid had to turn around and retrieve it before returning the pass.

I thought, if the immobility of the top hand gums up passing, how about receiving? Sure enough. The only hand that moved on a reception was the bottom hand, with the top hand locked on the hip as a

87

88

swivel point. How could the boy move it? If he brought the top hand six inches forward to clear the hip, with his stick too long, the toe of the blade lifted three inches off the ice. (87) And if he moved top hand and bottom hand together to keep the blade square with the oncoming pass, he had to move the top hand right through his body. (88)

Well, most kids insist on using sticks that are too long, and coaches across the country let them do it. So how do you teach the masses to receive a pass with a stick that is too long? We had the answer for that one all the time and didn't know it. Roll the wrists. We found that by rolling the wrist toward the oncoming pass the toe of the blade comes in, keeping the puck from running off the blade, and the heel goes out, absorbing the puck's impact.

Then after working on it for a while we had the player go out several inches to meet the approaching puck and not give at all with the lower hand at the moment of impact. He simply rolled his wrists so that the toe cradled the puck and the heel absorbed the energy.

The boys, meantime, were coming along with each step as we worked it out together, and many of them were really getting the idea. Normally during passing drills, the arena is as noisy as the inside of a boiler with a riveting machine working on the outside. I remember moving in beside one boy to give him some advice, shouting at the top of my voice. The youngster almost jumped out of his jockstrap and so did I.

Why scream? The noise had almost died out and you could carry on a conversation in a normal voice. The boys were completely absorbed in learning. Although I still had the problem of motivating them for the passing drills that came later, I could now run drills that wouldn't disturb a funeral service in the bleachers.

And thanks to a strangely inspired thought in the interior of Newfoundland, I now had a new understanding of the art of passing. So let's start teaching it.

Vision

When I use the term *split vision* in teaching, I'm really referring to peripheral vision—what a car driver uses when his eyes look straight down the road but he can still see a car coming out of a side street beside him. Split vision only reinforces confidence in, or confirms what your hands tell you about, the position of the puck.

For without feel, you're included in the 85% of all hockey players who take their eyes off the target, look down at the puck, and when they know where it is, shoot or pass from memory. When a player looks down at the puck, a defender is on his way to the target before the puck is, or the goal tender is moving to close the angle before the puck is shot.

What would your reaction be if while watching a hunter walk across a field, a pheasant rose and the hunter brought the gun to his shoulder, lined up on the bird and before squeezing the trigger— looked down at his shoes? Don't laugh. You are probably one of the bunch who pass and shoot from memory.

Everyone can develop his peripheral or split vision (unless he has one of several eye defects that retard it) to the point where he will not have to look down at the puck, but will still see enough of it to confirm its location. I had a very bad case of 'tunnel vision', but overcame it by skating with the puck, looking at one point at the end of the arena, and then trying to identify other things toward the outside of my field of view. Just look up from this book, stare at your wife or sister sitting at the end of the chesterfield, and without moving your focal point, try to see the cushion (and its colour) at the other end of the chesterfield. See what I mean? After a few tries you can even follow the course of the cushion she chucks at you for staring at her without seeing her.

By now I have so much confidence in my feel of the puck that I hardly use my split vision.

Teaching the Sense of Feel
The most important sense to be developed for passing is that of feel. A player must acquire complete confidence in what his hands tell him. When the puck is stickhandled and cradled by the blade, it sends a message up the stick that the hands can feel and translate. The hands can tell the player exactly where that puck is—at the toe, heel or in the centre of the blade in the passing or shooting position. The kid who masters this sense of feeling the puck with his hands will never have to worry about being a good puck handler or passer. He will be half way there.

The players must be convinced that they can really feel the puck and get to know where it is on the stick at all times. I can demonstrate it, but a great many coaches will not be able to; in that case they will have to give verbal inspiration until someone on the squad picks it up and can show how it's done.

Stand in the stickhandling position and demonstrate. Look ahead at the tallest boy's helmet and stickhandle the puck, speaking this kind of patter: "Now it's on the heel of my stick, and now it's on the toe. Now it's in the shooting or passing position, and now it's back on the heel. Now I want to pass the puck, so I have to get it in the middle of the blade. Now it's on the toe, and now back to the middle."

Your eyes do not leave the player's helmet at any time during the stickhandling, and the puck is always where you say it is on the blade of your stick. They're pretty impressed by this time, but then you spring the clincher. Stop the puck at any position in front of you and straighten up, still looking at the kid's helmet, raise your stick high in the air above your shoulders, turn the toe down and put the point of the stick right on top of the puck.

They're bug-eyed. Then I repeat the exercise for a minute or so, giving a running commentary on where the puck is on my stick, stop, raise my stick and land on the puck again. Well, eight or nine times out of ten I can find it without ever looking down, and the kids get a great charge out of it when I miss. But they sure know it can be done, and have something to measure up to.

Then, make everyone take off their gloves (because most boys' gloves have palm leather so thick they couldn't feel a jackhammer vibrate), give each of them a puck and line half of them up on the red line, the other half on the blue line. Pair them off so they look across at their partner's helmet. Get them into the stickhandling position and start them off hollering "heel . . . toe . . . middle . . . " and so on. With their bare hands on the stick, they will quickly get the message from the puck, but it will take them a while to translate it into a puck position. You'll see an awful lot of peeking.

Then blow the whistle to stop the action, make them straighten up, put their sticks up in the air and bring them down square on the puck. Doggone it, some of them do.

Then put them through it again, trying to make sure they keep their eyes on their partners' helmets all the time. Make sure they keep the full blade of the stick on the ice. They usually get a kick out of this, because it turns into a contest when it comes time to put the point of the stick down on the puck.

Here we also have to start working on the maneuverability of the top hand. Most kids keep it frozen to their hip and can't move it from there, severely restricting all phases of puck handling, passing, receiving and shooting.

When doing the previous

89

90

exercise, make the players move the puck well out to the forehand. (89) This will cause them to bring the top hand out in front of the chest and well out to the backhand, (90) making them move the top hand four to six inches away from the hip. Unless they can perform the backhand exercise, they will never learn to pass backhand. (90)

For additional skill practice, have

the players skate slowly back and forth across the ice surface, stickhandling the puck while their eyes are level with the top of the boards opposite.

The next time you practice the puck handling drills, if the players are getting fairly proficient at pylon skating, make them look at the top of the next pylon as soon as they round the first. I add a little challenge to this drill by putting different coloured balls on the top of each pylon and making the player call out the colour as soon as he sees it.

Before we get to the passing drills, there is a more general problem that gets in the way of developing good passers in this country. It seems to me that when the players study under several coaches, there is no consistency either in teaching technique or game philosophy. The sooner we get some kind of standardized program that works in any part of the country, the sooner we will start producing the number and quality of hockey players that we can produce and that the present day market demands.

Passing Technique and Drills

Remember:
- It helps if the stick is the right length—about nine inches shorter than the player when he is on skates.
- It helps if the blade has a flat bottom—straight, not rockered.
- It helps if the blade is straight, or 'centre', not curved for a left or right shot.

Now explain that the blade should be at right angles to the target, and demonstrate. Set up a player as a receiver and have him present his blade as a target. The instructor takes the stickhandling position and shows what happens when a pass is started at the centre line of the body, when the blade is square with the target.

Start the pass slowly and stop the stick after four or five inches of travel, when the puck would normally disengage from the blade. Get another player to skate up behind your stick and give the blade a good, sharp kick right behind the puck. The pass will be at least two feet off target.

Now go through the same routine, but start the pass four to six inches behind the centre line of the body, in front of the rear feet. Again stop the stick and puck after six inches of travel, now at the centre line of the body, and get the player to kick the back of the stick again. The puck can't miss, because the blade should have been at right angles to the target when it stopped.

Demonstrate the technique of receiving. Show what happens if they intercept the puck at the centre line of the body, and the stick gives with the pass. The blade opens and the puck slides off. Then show them how to meet the puck several inches in front of the centre line, and how to roll the wrists when intercepting.

Drill 1—Forward Pass between Two Lines

Line up the players on the blue line and red line and pair them off. (91) They straddle the line, with one foot on the outside and the other on the inside. Each pair, one on the blue line and the other on the red line, should be pointing shoulder to shoulder.

They are now in the only position in which to learn how to pass the puck, i.e., by using the line as a guide. (92) By drawing the puck back over the outside edge of the line they will have it well behind centre of the body, (93) and the blade should be square with the target at the moment of release. (94)

The passers begin stickhandling the puck, keeping their eyes on their partners' stick blades. The partner presents his stick blade as a target, and the passer lets the puck go at medium speed. The receiver intercepts it, stickhandles it a few times

92

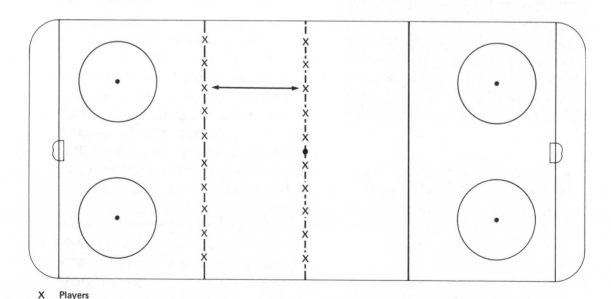

X   Players
→   Direction of passes

91

93

94

to get the feel, and passes the puck back again.

That's the way it is supposed to work.

Now look for, and correct these faults:

- Feet in the wrong position. They should be shoulder width, and lined up with the receiver.

- Hands not in the stickhandling or passing position, and the body hunched over the stick.
- Looking down at the puck while stickhandling.
- Looking down at the puck before passing.
- Receiving a pass, then letting the puck sit and slapping it back without stickhandling.
- Putting the puck in position, then looking at the target and passing.
- Passing too slowly or too quickly.
- The wise guy who thinks he knows it all and that this is beneath him.

The instructor must constantly check players for looking down at the puck before passing. The kids find the temptation to look almost irresistable, and, as long as they get away with it, will never get confidence in feel. The instructor will be doing the player the biggest favour by screaming blue murder every time he sees him look down at the puck.

The instructors will probably find it necessary to work at this drill in stages. They will have to concentrate on passing technique at first, and just get the receiver to present at target. Then they can concentrate on the receiver, checking his faults.

Backhand Passing

Now turn around and do this drill for backhand passing. A player can't make an accurate backhand pass until he moves the top hand away from the body. To do this he requires good balance to allow him to move his top hand three or four inches out from the body, and to move his bottom hand, shoulder and stick across the front of the body. A considerable amount of weight is shifted in a backhand pass, and unless a player is steady on his skates, he is in trouble.

The backhand pass works on the same principle as the forehand. If the pass is started at the centre line of the body, the puck will go into the receiver's skates. And if the pass is started behind the centre line, with the top hand on the hip as a swivel point, (95) the puck will roll off the end of the blade before the blade is square with the target, and go ahead of the receiver.

So there's only one answer. When ready to move the stick back of centre and pass, the player must move both hands out with the stick. (90) (96) When he draws back, the blade is square with the target. When he makes the pass the player

again moves both hands, and the blade is still square at the moment of puck release. If done properly, the puck has to be right on target.

Unfortunately, an explanation and demonstration at this point will probably not be enough for the lesson to sink in. The kid has enough to worry about—position of feet on the lines, position of hands, presenting or watching a target, stickhandling the puck (without peeking), and receiving the puck. When they're somewhere in that cycle, they can't tell you how many hands or feet they have, let alone remember to move the top hand away from the body when making a backhand pass.

Hardly more than one in 15 boys will pick up the backhand technique after one—or two—demonstrations. The only way is to stand beside each boy, put your hands on the stick with his, and go through the cycle with him. When he recognizes the feel of moving the top hand out he will be able to duplicate it, and

95

96

now you're on the right track.

Now look at the receivers. Are they rolling the wrists to compensate for the too-long stick?

Have the boys reach out several inches to meet the oncoming puck. The lower hand should not give at all at the moment of impact. (97) Look at (98)(99). Notice how the toe simply cradles the puck, and the heel absorbs the energy.

Then go back to the demonstrations and have the players follow along with you. They start to get it a lot faster now. Put them through the forehand pass, receiving, and the backhand pass. Stop every so often and demonstrate again. Now they're getting pretty good and you're starting to feel pretty good about it. So it's time to get them mobile and let the wind out of your sails.

Drill 2—Passing in Pairs

Set up the course with pylons, as in (100).

The players skate slowly around the outside of the rink in pairs, about ten or 12 feet apart. They repeat the same drill they were doing when standing still—stickhandling the puck, looking at the target, taking the puck back of centre and passing to the target. They change places with their partners at both ends of the rink, the inside man going outside and vice versa.

97

98

99

Problems? First of all they can't go slowly, or stay ten feet apart. They look at the puck, and most of them slap it back. There is never a target. On the end turns, the inside man gets way ahead of the outside man. And at the end where they change over, you need 16 traffic cops to keep order.

At this point I take them back to the standing drills for a couple of minutes, then to the moving drill, and if necessary, back to the standing drill again. They should now be ready for the next step.

The In Air Pass

Also called raising the puck. Don't confuse this with the *flip pass*, which never made sense to me. When a puck is flipped it usually flies through the air like a football from the kickoff. When it lands it bounces like crazy, making it almost impossible to receive and control.

For accuracy and control, a raised puck should return to the ice gently and nestle in like a glider landing on a foam rubber field. It should fly and land like a frisbee. What it needs is spin.

Start the pass using the normal technique, with the puck on the heel of the stick. Roll the wrists during the sweep and by the time the puck has travelled from the heel to the centre of the blade and disengages, it should have a really fast spin. Then it will sail through the air and return to the ice surface gently, still flat.

Now go back to *Drill 1*, and, lay boards on the ice midway between the passers and receivers. The boards I use are about two inches by one inch, and I keep them in place with sandbags. The players practise raising the puck back and forth to each other, over the boards.

The players should first practise

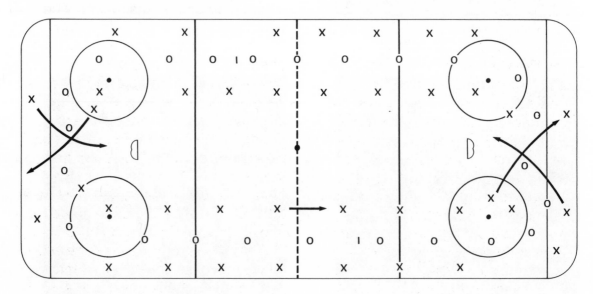

O   Pylons
X   Players
I   Instructor

this skill by using a puck with the crest upward, trying to impart as much spin as possible in a short distance.

Later they can practise raising the puck when skating slowly forward, passing the puck straight ahead to a target.

Drill 3–Skating in Pairs with Obstacles

This drill is the same as *Drill 2* but with overturned pylons and boards added to the course. (100) The players skate around the course using the forehand and backhand pass, avoiding the pylons, and raising the puck over the boards where they are placed.

Drill 4–Passing in Pairs, in Three Areas

Now we are getting closer to game conditions. Divide the ice into three zones and put five pairs of players in each. Scatter boards and overturned pylons throughout the zones. The pairs skate anywhere they like within the zone, passing back and forth to each other. They should stay close together and the instructor should insist on short, sharp passes aimed at the blade of the receiver's stick.

Play a game—get the pass receiver to stop or change direction if he sees the passer look down before making the pass. Then when the passer looks up again his receiver is somewhere else, grinning like a Cheshire cat.

What usually happens in this drill

is that the players go too fast and get too far apart. To take full advantage of the boards and pylons scattered in each zone they should make slow, controlled sweeps of their zone.

Drill 5–Passing Course

This drill, moving another step closer to game conditions, is by far the best, and my favourite. I could play it all day long but the kids would rather scrimmage. So the problem was motivation. I found that the occasional free soft drink and a more expensive incentive later on worked wonders. The older, more experienced players are best at this drill, but it helps everyone gain more confidence.

Let's look at the layout in (101). The circles are pylons, the targets are numbered *1* to *8*, and the crosses represent the passers and the pass retrievers. The latter, with about six pucks each, are beside each target. During the drill they gather up the loose pucks and feed them back to the passers.

Now we have one player standing by each target, whose job it is to feed passes back to the players going through the course. The rest of the players line up and the first one starts from the goal line. His first pass to the first target must be a forward pass, so he has to make his move just after he reaches the first pylon. If he is right handed, he will make this pass on his backhand, if left handed, on his forehand. A right-handed player will make

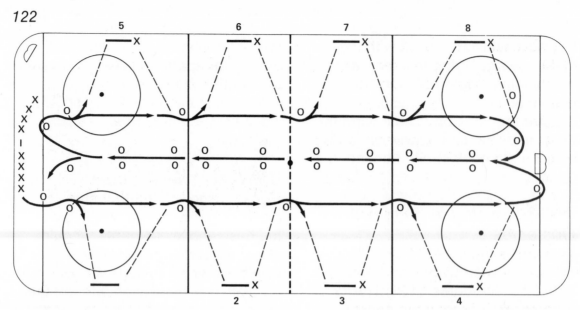

O   Pylons
X   Players
I   Instructor

101

passes 5 to 8 on his forehand, a
left-handed player on his backhand.
As soon as he makes his pass he
must get ready to receive a return
pass from the player beside the
target.

When the moving player takes the
return pass, he skates for a couple
of strides until he reaches the next
pylon, and makes another forward
pass at that target. When he
reaches the last target and takes a
return pass, he comes back up the
centre ice lane for his try at four
forehand passes.

The second player starts through
the course when the first has taken
his first return pass.

After five minutes of this, rotate
the players so that those standing at
the targets get their turn through the
course.

The trouble starts with the
backhand passes. No one gets
anywhere near the target and you

have to go back to square one in
backhand passing. The players will
have to understand that in order to
make a forward pass backhand they
have to shift feet. In order to get the
blade of the stick square with a
target ahead of the body, the bottom
hand must come right across the
front and the top hand move well
away from the body. When making
backhand lateral passes standing
still, players have most success with
their weight evenly divided on both
feet and their shoulders pointed at
the target. But now, with the target
in front of the body, a player must
swivel his hips and shoulders to
help line up on the target. It takes
time and patience for them to adjust
to the backhand forward pass when
moving.

You know that the first time
through this drill it is going to break
down completely at some point. The
moving passers break every rule

they have learned. But they must be made to do it right. The kids will test the coach to the Nth degree, but once they understand that the practice part of the day is yours and the game is theirs, the situation gets better.

With so many things going on at the same time, and so many teaching situations arising, the coach and instructors simply can't keep track of everyone. At first I kept feeling that too many players were just going through the motions, so with not enough instructors to watch everyone, I needed some motivation.

Now, when starting the passing course drill, I pin a ten dollar bill to the top of the glass at one end of the rink, with a clothes pin. Any player who hits the four targets on the first half of the course presses a loud buzzer that is used for changing lines in minor league games. Then everybody stops to watch him in the last half of the course because if he hits seven out of eight, he gets the ten dollar bill and the rest of the team gets a free soft drink.

Well, I haven't lost more than two ten dollar bills yet but I sure would like to. So far, in several years of trying, only two players and I have hit the seven mark. But now, most of the guys can't wait to get on the passing course.

When the players learn the routine of the passing course and get the hang of the passing technique, it's time to make it a little tougher. Set the boards out again,

102

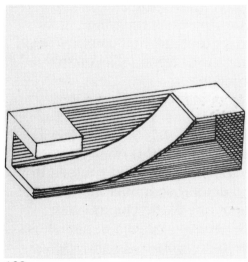

103   *Box tipped on back edge*

and make them raise a pass at the target over the boards. You can bring out the boards for the passers standing at the targets, sooner than you can for the moving passers.

The targets went through some modifications before we arrived at the one you see in (102) (103). Initially, the long, rectangular box was made of metal, and the puck was fired into the open front, then bounced up through the open ceiling, sometimes as high as 20 feet into the air.

Because of the obvious dangers with flying pucks, the revised version was made of wood, with an open front, closed roof, and one side open—four opened at the left side for one side of the rink, four at the right side for the other side.

To slow down the progress of the puck, we covered the open end with a thick rubber flap, attached at its top end only. When finished, we had a unique target box, testing the boys' ability to fire the puck inside it, and saving endless time for the passers in retrieving flying pucks.

It's a great drill that can be a lot of fun for the players . . . if you make it interesting.

Drill 6—Passing on a Circle

To demonstrate this one, get your three best passers and yourself to stand equally spaced around the edge of one of the circles. With skates outside the circle, and sticks on it, the players try to stay in the same spot through the drill.

The idea is to stickhandle the puck once and pass it to another player of your choice on the circle, forehand or backhand. The key is thinking.

The receiver has to show the passer the full blade of his stick, and it must be presented at a different angle every time the puck is passed. When the receiver takes a pass he handles it once and passes it in turn to someone else. Let the players on the circle practise this for a few minutes until they pick up the routine, and then start adding pressure.

Put a checker inside the circle to chase and intercept the puck. When he does block a pass, the passer takes the checker's place inside the circle. You can work five boys in every circle, and make a sixth circle in the centre ice area with pylons.

Now, with the checker applying pressure to the passers on the circle, its just like game conditions. The passer must keep his head up and stickhandle once. If his sense of feel is good he knows where the puck is on his stick. And if has worked on his split—or peripheral—vision, he can watch the checker and see his four receivers. He should see on which side the checker has his stick, and whether the checker's skates are apart or closed. If there are four passers with heads up, the checker should never get close to the puck. Don't leave the same checker in too long, and try to balance each circle with players of equal ability.

Of course you know what happens when you first add a checker to a smoothly operating circle. Panic. Once again every rule and skill goes out the window. They drop their heads, forget to handle the puck but slap it instead. They pass forehand only, and forget to roll the wrists when receiving. But, thank God, they learn to play it cool under pressure, and eventually 65% of the players will show marked improvement.

The circle passing game creates a teaching situation for a problem that plagues all our hockey players at every level—putting themselves in check.

So many players move into a position on the ice which makes it impossible for a team mate to pass the puck without passing it through or very close to a defender.

An attacking player without the puck should always head for open ice, with no defenceman or checker between the passer and the receiver.

When passing on a circle, it's easy to show the players that they can uncheck themselves or become a potential pass receiver simply by moving the stick from the forehand to the backhand.

6
Goal Tending

This past summer I was lucky enough to acquire the services of Buddy Blom to teach basic goal tending techniques to the young goalers who attended my hockey school in Stanstead, Quebec. Buddy holds a Masters degree in teaching, and is presently working in a high school in Colorado. He played goal for Hamilton Juniors when they last won the Memorial Cup, and after a university career in Colorado, played minor professional. Bud is a rare fellow, able to teach skills at the level demanded by the pupil—and at most hockey schools, that means the ABC's, not XYZ's. He can relate to kids of any age and talks the language they understand, So, over the summer, we talked goal tending at every opportunity—the next few pages are thoughts I wrote down after many a happy evening talking goal tending with Buddy Blom.

Great Goalers are Made

It seems that most kids get started in goal almost by accident, as did some of the greatest goalers in recent years. Terry Sawchuck inherited his pads from an older brother—so did Ed Giacomin and Dave and Ken Dryden. Les Binkley was a trainer at a time when trainers were expected to be practice goalers because the clubs in those days only carried one goaler. Glenn Hall was the best skater and leading scorer on his school team when his goaler quit. No one else would play goal, so young Hall ended up in the nets and did so well that a Detroit scout signed him.

The odds are that Tony Esposito started in goal because his older brother Phil wanted somebody to pelt shots at and Tony was too stubborn to say "No."

The stories go on and on. One factor keeps recurring, however, whether a Sawchuck, Hall or Esposito—every goaler who ever made the N.H.L. and stuck, possessed, besides courage, great skating ability.

Only the Best Skaters

Ironically enough, most young goalers, or would-be goalers nine to 12 years of age, end up in the nets because they have a natural desire to play, crave the peer group solidarity of the game—and just happen to be the poorest skaters in their age group. To keep from getting yelled at, they go into goal, where they soon gain the respect of their 'buddies' just for having the courage to stand there while their friends (ha) fire away.

You see, he can't lose. If he's bad, all the guys on the other side butter him up so he won't quit. They naturally want to keep scoring. If he's good, he has the admiration of his own team mates. Naturally he prefers that and tries to excel.

O.K., for whatever reason, your son is a goal tender. Naturally, to keep his buddies' respect, as their abilities increase, he must increase his own.

Right back at square one, aren't we? If the poor little duffer can't skate, and doesn't improve his skating, you can be sure of one then pay the price. About $200 will get him goal skates, pads, gloves, shoulder, arm and stomach pads, jockstrap and cup, pants, mask and stick.

I've seen so many parents buy full equipment, then, for some unknown reason, balk at buying goal skates. Holy Jumping Catfish, you're protecting everything but the most vulnerable spot. Without the proper foot and ankle protection, he will develop bad habits he can never undo. The boy will be afraid to turn his foot outward to expose the inside of his foot on low shots to the corner. Consequently, he won't be moving his body into the shot or into the direction the puck is headed. If he doesn't learn this important skill at an early age, he probably never will. There goes his chance of being a good goaler.

Questions Goalers Ask

Budding goalers are always asking me: how would I stop a breakaway? How should I stop a screened shot? What do you do on a deflection? When should I move out? How do you tell what the attacker is going to do? I could tell them all kinds of things beginning with " . . . well, it depends on the situation."

How fast is the attacker moving on the breakaway? Is he coming straight at you or from an angle? Where are you in the net? Is anyone coming back to help you?

But you know what? It's a wasted effort on my part to teach a boy how to play goal at this time, unless he is (here we go again) an excellent

Goaler equipment.

Ken Dryden makes the save.

skater, stands on his feet and keeps his stick on the ice. If he can't do these things, he can't make the necessary move to cancel out the attacker's scoring effort.

I look at a young goaler and ask him to do one thing before anything else: let's see you skate, son. And I don't mean skate forward or skate without pads. He must skate in full equipment. I get him on a face-off circle and have him skate forward and backward both ways. I look for one thing in particular: can he get the outside leg over the inside leg without losing his balance?

One thing seems to recur time and time again. A boy can go one way fairly well, but he looks like a dog running on a slick pond, going the other way. That's not strange when you stop to think about it. How many of us can write or throw equally well with either hand, kick equally well with either foot, hit successfully from either side of home plate? The answer is obvious. We all tend to favour one side or the other. And yet, if the need arises, we can be taught to perform equally with either hand or foot.

I recently saw some statistics: seven out of ten goals are scored along the ice, one out of ten is scored above the knee. That makes sense. We naturally do things better with our hands than with our feet. Further, the width of the body covers more net, a high shot is closer to a goaler's eye—you can see why a save is easier to make above the knee.

Most goals then should be scored

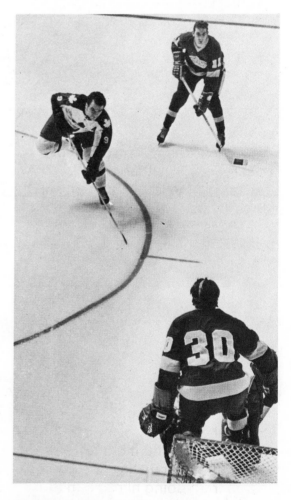

A breakaway situation.

for every raggedy-assed kid with mail order catalogue shin pads who learns to skate on a frozen pond should be demolished. So must the impression created by teams of "Superstar Peewees" which draw attention away from where it rightfully belongs—with thousands of minor league teams that are learning hockey at a normal pace.

What the professionals do with the game is their problem. But when professional attitudes are pushed into adolescents who then expect to become overnight bonus babies, it's a problem that should concern everyone in the country who is interested in amateur hockey.

So let's ease off on the pushing and let young hockey players concentrate on the game basics. Let them have fun until they are physically and emotionally ready to chase the dollar sign. In the long run it will give the professionals, and the country's disappointed television fans, enough talent to take on any challenger, Russian or otherwise.